Architectural Precedents
Historic Case Studies on Spatial Density and Seclusion

Edited by Rubén Alcolea

faber
press

Published in the United States by Faber Press

Library of Congress
Cataloging-in-Publication Data

Alcolea, Rubén (editor)
Architectural Precedents. Historic Case Studies
on Spatial Density and Seclusion
Rhode Island: Faber Press, 2025
ISBN 979-8-99880370-3 hardback
ISBN 979-8-99880371-0 ebook
ISBN 979-8-99880372-7 paperback

NA2699.NA350.NA4850
1. Alcolea, Rubén
2. Architectural drawing and design
3. Architectural study and teaching
4. Castles and monasteries

10 9 8 7 6 5 4 3 2 1

Designed by Faber Press
First Edition

Architectural Precedents
Historic Case Studies
on Spatial Density and
Seclusion

Precedents
by **Rubén Alcolea**

It is well known how young Le Corbusier was strongly influenced by his visit to the Acropolis in Athens. His journey went beyond Athens, traveling around the ancient Mediterranean world in a personal quest for what he described as the "fundamentals of architecture".[1] The early works by the Swiss born architect had strong resonance with the vernacular, and he seemed committed to defining a clear connection–even a logical one–between modernism and the classics. His attentive study of the work by Palladio, for example, is only one of the multiple examples in his intellectual journey to try a definition of the essence of architecture beyond the pure formalization of stylistic language.[2] The early sketches he produced while visiting the ruins of Greek and Roman constructions or of the monastic cells at the Monastery of Ema left a deep footprint in his way of thinking about architecture, not only as an expression of modern times or new construction technologies but, more importantly, as an intellectual and spatial exercise which would need to have the ability to keep its value over time while projecting it into the future. One can hear more than just an echo of the Acropolis while visiting the Chapel of Notre-Dame du Haut in Ronchamp, as the precise placement of the building in the landscape and the sequenced path to get there do not differ too much from those in Athens. It would be argued that Le Corbusier looked ahead to the future of architecture with the same intensity as he was looking back to its past. Perhaps that may be why in many of his late works– and in Chandigarh in particular–the extensive use of rough concrete and expressive formalizations point to the realization of his dream to reconcile modernity, tradition, and artistic expression. During this time, he set aside the rigidity and strict parameters of the then-exhausted functionalist approach, opting instead for a powerful symbolism that drew on connections to ancient and primitive structures. There are many hidden cross-references–whether intentional or implied–in Le Corbusier's work, as if the architect tried to simultaneously define the essence of modern architecture while attentively looking back to its origins through history.

To a certain extent, all major modern architects have looked back at history to define the foundations of their own narrative. Louis Kahn also had a personal affinity towards architectural works from the past. His personal interest in several Scottish castles, for example, is well documented. Those constructions had an important influence on works such as the Exeter Library or the Assembly Building in Dacca, among many others. He made a flying visit to Scotland to visit castles in March 1961–while in London for another job while in the midst of the Erdman design–[3] and he very eloquently expressed the influence that those medieval structures had in his work. He wrote "The Scottish Castle. Thick, thick walls. Little openings to the enemy. Splayed inwardly to the occupant. A place to read, a place to sew… Places for the bed, for the stair… Sunlight".[4] It is difficult not to think about the beautiful drawings of Scottish castles while looking at projects developed right after that trip, such as his project for a chemistry building at the University of Virginia or his proposal for the Lawrence Memorial Hall of Science Competition. Actually, he admitted the influence while being asked about it in many occasions: "I have a book on castles and I try to pretend that I did not look at this book, but everybody reminds me of it and I have to admit that I looked very thoroughly at this book".[5] We have to acknowledge that there is a myth about the drawings of those castles, which while they are referred

as produced by Louis Kahn himself. The drawings attributed to Louis Kahn are in fact the ones which were originally published in the books he had.[6] In any case, the plans of Dover, Orford, and Borthwick castles were indeed influential. They serve as an important reference for understanding not only his work, but also more recent practices, particularly those derived from the work of Louis Kahn. In these cases, we see a consistent and deliberate use of basic geometry, an emphasis on mass and heaviness, and a high degree of abstraction. Louis Kahn looked at the medieval structures as generative diagrams, able to be reinterpreted or reused within other projects despite their program or location. It is also known that Louis Kahn had the book *Castles from the Air* by W. Douglas Simpson, and the author pointed that looking at those precedents from a distant bird's eye view revealed new aspects only visible while seeing them as a whole. "Air photography reveals them to us in a new aspect. The whole ordaining of the building, the devising and balance of its masses, the way in which it is fitted to its site, the articulation of masonry, earthwork and water defenses, the happy marriage between mansion and gardens, the whole way in which a great house, or a shattered ruin, sits into its surrounding–all these can now be studied from an angle, at once physical and mental, not hitherto available".[7] It is interesting to note that despite the fact that castles and defensive structures are by their own nature generally very compact, efficient, and self-referenced, the author suggests that there is a certain particular and subtle fit to the surroundings, sometimes evidenced by a slight tilt in its organization in plan, a distinct way of approaching the building, or through an exception, a break in its symmetrical configuration to dialog with a topographical

1. This trip was essential in writing his seminal text Voyage d'Orient. Many scholars have discussed about this. For a more recent conversation see William JR Curtis, "The Classical Ideals of Le Corbusier," Architectural Review (blog), September 21, 2011.

2. A deep analysis on the work of Le Corbusier in relation to the work of Palladio can be found in Colin Rowe, "The Mathematics of the Ideal Villa," in The Mathematics of the Ideal Villa, and Other Essays (Cambridge, Mass.: MIT Press, 1976), 1–27; and in Barry Maitland, "The Grid," Oppositions, no. 15/16 (1979): 90–117.

3. David Gilson De Long and David B. Brownlee, eds., Louis I. Kahn: In the Realm of Architecture (New York: Rizzoli, 1991), p. 165.

4. Quote extracted from a letter from Louis Kahn to Richard Demarco, August 28, 1973. Cited in David Gilson De Long and David B. Brownlee, eds., Louis I. Kahn: In the Realm of Architecture (New York: Rizzoli, 1991), p. 107.

5. Cited in David Gilson De Long and David B. Brownlee, eds., Louis I. Kahn: In the Realm of Architecture (New York: Rizzoli, 1991), p. 165. Peter S. Reed suggests that the book was probably Williams Douglas Simpson, Castles from the Air. Alexandra Tyng notes that in 1962 he was given Stewart Cruden, The Scottish Castle.

6. David MacGibbon and Thomas Ross, The Castellated and Domestic Architecture of Scotland from the Twelfth to the Eighteenth Century, 5 vols. (Edinburgh: D. Douglas, 1887).

7. William Douglas Simpson, Castles from the Air (London: Country Life, 1949), p. 9.

8. In Western philosophy and literature, the Myth of the Noble Savage refers to a stock character who is uncorrupted by civilization. As such, the "noble" savage symbolizes the innate goodness and moral superiority of a primitive people living in harmony with nature. This concept can be found in literary works by John Dryden and Charles Dickens, although it was mostly developed by Jean-Jacques Rousseau in its philosophical texts.

9. Rubén Alcolea and Jorge Tárrago "Somewhere in our Memory," in Práctica arquitectónica III : Architectural practice III, ed. Daniel Gimeno and Guitart, Miguel, 1a ed. (Buenos Aires: Nobuko, 2017), pp. 22–50.

feature. The balance between the radical and clear autonomy of the built object and its subtle dialog with the environment–particularly in terms of scale or location–is what has captivated so many modern architects. The reference to medieval constructions, monasteries, and fortifications are necessary to understand not only the works of Louis Kahn but also the production of many other contemporary architects. Similar principles to the ones used by Kahn in his late works are visible in recent projects by major figures such as Peter Zumthor, Valerio Olgiati, Roger Bolthauser, or Aires Mateus, and are still playing an important role in the education and practice of new generations of architects.

The use of historical precedents as references has been widely used in modern and contemporary practices. Even during the vibrant and radical first moments of the avant-garde. When it was necessary to define and clarify the modern ideals, architects and artists looked back with sharp eyes to architectures which had been able to keep its value and significance through time. As of today, schools of architecture continue the widespread practice of inducing students to find appropriate precedents, helping them clarify their design intentions and serving as a guide throughout the creative process. And although the appropriateness of those references may not always be clear to them or even valid to their instructors' eyes, what matters most is that architecture should always look for sources, in one way or another. The possibility of actually designing from scratch does not seem realistic, as there is no such thing such as a Noble Savage in architecture.[8] But every architect and designer, even students or the ones at the beginning of their careers, have been necessarily exposed to precedents of different sorts, which have permeated to create the set of references to be called upon subconsciously while engaging in the design process. While the concept of originality in architecture is a topic broadly discussed in many other volumes,[9] we could still say that it is dangerous to pretend that a project can be fully original or innovative by itself. Current computer-aided processes, including what is now commonly referred to as artificial Intelligence (AI), exist precisely because of the vast amount of prior knowledge and content from where they are trained. The machine creates not so differently than us, by collaging, combining, making relationships, or variations on pre-existing texts, images or data structures. It is by producing the unexpected, which is usually brought by the machine as another variation with more severe transformations, where both the machine and the human mind surprise us the most. It is then our task to critically evaluate the consistency and pertinence of these new not-so-original ideas, by acknowledging its intrinsic genealogy and find its current value and suitability as one more step in the infinite sequence of variations embedded in any creative process.

This volume does not pretend to provide sources for generating architecture, and even less to identify the more compelling or valid ones. It is not a history book on medieval fortresses, either. It simply looks back to a few medieval and historic structures—castles and monasteries in particular—where some basic principles of architectural composition become clear and transparent through the lens of newly produced homogeneous drawings. It may be that the distance in time to those works gives us a sort of naked and idealized version of what all those constructions wanted to be, or what we may have wanted them to be. Each precedent is presented with similar graphics, providing essential information such as aerial/satellite photographs, site plans,

their accurate location, and a very brief text. The descriptions are not so much about their history, but more so to point out some of the universal architecture principles which they showcase, such as structure, composition, symmetry, scale, or sequence, among many others. Each precedent is followed by a relatively large plan and section, detailed to some extent, though not enough to provide a fully accurate or precise depiction either of their current state or their primitive form. Plans and drawings aim to provide–with realistic scale and proportions–an open-ended version of the idealized precedent. An out-of-scale detail of a fragment is then presented, simplified either in plan or in section, followed by an abstract geometric representation of one of the architectural principles distilled from its study. Both the detailed and abstract geometric drawings aim to open the door to a deeper understanding of the precedent. They invite interpretations that, while perhaps absent at the time of construction, now emerge as prompts for continued exploration in architectural thought. The selection of precedents is both arbitrary and intentional. For example, many of the Scottish castles that inspired Louis Kahn are included in this volume. Their strong geometric nature slightly contrasts the selected Spanish fortresses, which tend to generally be more layered and less compact. Finally, a set of monasteries from eastern latitudes provide a different look at how some of those constructions dealt intimately with landscape and topography in a few extreme and beautiful locations while acknowledging the values of seclusion and isolation. Overall, this book offers drawings to look at, hoping that some of them will inform the creation of new projects or the reflection on existing ones.

Michel de Montaigne (1533-1592) was one of the most important philosophers during the French Renaissance. He really championed the solo existence. He was a lawyer and a civil servant until he himself retired from public life at the age of 38, locking himself away in near total reclusion in a tower in his Château, to contemplate the nature of things. It was then when he wrote his famous 'Essays'. In his essay 39, On Solitude, he reflects on the very nature of human existence, advocating by a gradual removal of ourselves from all the ties which bind.

Original Text: Essay 39: On Solitude, by Michel de Montaigne, Cotton, Charles, Carew Hazlitt, William (Ed.), Essays of Michel de Montaigne. London: Templeman, 1877, Volume 6

Let us leave aside the usual long comparison between the solitary and the active life; and as for that fine statement under which ambition and avarice take cover–that we are not born for our private selves, but for the public–let us boldly appeal to those who are in the midst of the dance. Let them cudgel their conscience and say whether, on the contrary, the titles, the offices, and the hustle and bustle of the world are not sought out to gain private profit from the public. The evil means men use in our day to push themselves show clearly that the end is not worth much. Let us reply to ambition that it is she herself that gives us a taste for solitude. For what does she shun so much as society? What does she seek so much as elbowroom? There is opportunity everywhere for doing good or evil. However, if Bias' statement is true, that the wicked are in the majority, or what Ecclesiastes says, that not one in a thousand is good–

The good are rare: if all their numbers you compile, They'll scarcely match the gates of Thebes, the mouths of Nile. (Juvenal)

–contagion is very dangerous in the crowd. One must either imitate the vicious or hate them. Both these things are dangerous: to imitate them because they are many, and to hate many of them because they are unlike us.

Merchants who go to sea are right to be careful that those who embark on the same ship are not dissolute, blasphemous, or wicked, and to regard such company as unlucky. Wherefore Bias said humorously to those who were undergoing with him the danger of a great tempest and calling on the gods for help: "Be quiet, so they may not realize that you are here with me." And in a more pressing case, Albuquerque, viceroy in the Indies for King Manuel of Portugal, when in great peril of shipwreck at sea, took a young boy upon his shoulders for this purpose alone, that in their common danger the boy's innocence might serve him as a guarantee and a recommendation to divine favor, and bring him to safety.

It is not that the wise man cannot live anywhere content, yes, and alone in a palace crowd; but if he has the choice, says he, he will flee even the sight of a throng. He will endure it, if need be, but if it is up to him, he will choose solitude. He does not feel sufficiently rid of vices if he must still contend with those of other men. Charondas chastised as evil those who were convicted of keeping evil company.

There is nothing so unsociable and so sociable as man; the one by his vice, the other by his nature. And Antisthenes does not seem to me to have given a satisfactory answer to the man who reproached him for associating with wicked men, when he said that doctors lived well enough among the sick; for if they improve the health of the sick, they impair their own by contagion, and by the constant sight and treatment of diseases.

Now the aim of all solitude, I take it, is the same: to live more at leisure and at one's ease. But people do not always look for the right way. Often they think they have left business, and they have only changed it. There is scarcely less trouble in governing a family than in governing an entire state: whatever the mind is wrapped up in, it is all wrapped up in it, and domestic occupations are no less importunate for being less important. Furthermore, by getting rid of the court and the market place we do not get rid of the principal worries of our life:

Reason and sense remove anxiety,
Not villas that look out upon the sea. (Horace)

Ambition, avarice, irresolution, fear, and lust do not leave us when we change our country. *Behind the horseman sits black care.* (Horace)

They often follow us even into the cloisters and the schools of philosophy. Neither deserts, nor rocky caves, nor hair shirts, nor fastings will free us of them:

The fatal shaft sticks in her side. (Virgil)

Someone said to Socrates that a certain man had grown no better by his travels. "I should think not," he said; "he took himself along with him."

Why should we move to find
Countries and climates of another kind?
What exile leaves himself behind? (Horace)

If a man does not first unburden his soul of the load that weighs upon it, movement will cause it to be crushed still more, as in a ship the cargo is less cumbersome when it is settled. You do a sick man more harm than good by moving him. You imbed the malady by disturbing it, as stakes penetrate deeper and grow firmer when you budge them and shake them. Wherefore it is not enough to have gotten away from the crowd, it is not enough to move; we must get away from the gregarious instincts that are inside us, we must sequester and repossess ourselves.

"At last", you'll say, "I've snapped my chains."
A fleeing dog may well have snapped his, at great pains, Yet dangling from his neck the greater part remains. (Persius)

We take or chains along with us; our freedom is not complete; we still turn our eyes to what left behind, our fancy is full of it.

Unless the heart is purged, what must we undergo! / What battles and what perils, to our fruitless woe! / How great the bitter cares of lust that rend apart, / With terrors in their train, an agitated heart! / What ruin, what disasters, follow in the path / Of pride, and lust, and luxury, and sloth, and wrath!
(Lucretius)

Our illness grips us by the soul, and the soul cannot escape from itself:

The soul's at fault, which ne'er escapes itself.
(Horace)

Therefore we must bring it back and withdraw it into itself: that is the real solitude, which may be enjoyed in the midst of cities and the courts of kings; but it is enjoyed more handily alone.

Now since we are undertaking to live alone and do without company, let us make our contentment depend on ourselves; let us cut loose from all the ties that bind us to others; let us win from ourselves the power to live really alone and to live that way at our ease.

After Stilpo escaped the burning of his city, in which he had lost wife, children, and property, Demetrius Poliorcetes, seeing him unperturbed in expression amid the great ruin of his country, asked him if he had not suffered loss. No, he replied; thanks to God he had lost nothing of his own. The philosopher Antisthenes expressed the same idea humorously: that man should furnish himself with provisions that would float on water and could swim ashore with him from a shipwreck.

Certainly a man of understanding has lost nothing, if he has himself. When the city of Nola was ruined by the barbarians, Paulinus, the bishop of the city, who had lost everything and had been taken prisoner, prayed God thus: "Lord, keep me from feeling this loss; for Thou knowest that they have yet touched nothing of what is mine." The riches that made him rich and the goods that made him good were still entire. That is what it is to choose wisely the treasures that can be secured from harm, and to hide them in a place where no one may go and which can be betrayed only by ourselves.

We should have wife, children, goods, and above all health, if we can; but we must not bind ourselves to them so strongly that our happiness depends on them. We must reserve a back shop all our own, entirely free, in which to establish our real liberty and our principal retreat and solitude. Here our ordinary conversation must be between us and ourselves, and so private that no outside association or communication can find a place; here we must talk and laugh as if without wife, without children, without possessions, without retinue and servants, so that, when the time comes to lose them, it will be nothing new to us to do without them. We have a soul that can be turned upon itself; it can keep itself company; it has the means to attack and the means to defend, the means to receive and the means to give: let us not fear that in this solitude we shall stagnate in tedious idleness:

In solitude to be thyself a throng. (Tibullus)

Virtue, says Antisthenes, is content with itself, without rules, without words, without deeds. Among our customary actions there is not one in a thousand that concerns ourselves. The man you see climbing atop the ruins of that wall, frenzied and beside himself, a mark for so many harquebus shots; and that other, all scarred, pale and faint with hunger, determined to die rather than open the gates

to him-do you think they are there for their own sake? They are there for the sake of a man whom perhaps they never saw, who is not in the least concerned about their doings, and who at that very moment is plunged in idleness and pleasures.

This fellow, all dirty, with running nose and eyes, whom you see coming out of his study after midnight, do you think he is seeking among his books how to make himself a better, happier, and wiser man? No such news. He is going to teach posterity the meter of Plautus' verses and the true spelling of a Latin word, or die in the attempt. Who does not willingly exchange health, rest, and life for reputation and glory, the most useless, worthless, and false coin that is current among us? Our own death does not frighten us enough? Let us burden ourselves also with that of our wives, our children, and our servants. Our own affairs don't give us enough trouble? Let us also torment ourselves and get headaches over those of our neighbors and friends.

What! Shall a man establish in his soul, or prize. Anything dearer than himself in his own eyes? (Terence)

Solitude seems to me more appropriate and reasonable for those who have given to the world their most active and flourishing years, following the example of Thales. We have lived enough for others; let us live at least this remaining bit of life for ourselves. Let us bring back our thoughts and plans to ourselves and our well-being. It is no small matter to arrange our retirement securely; it keeps us busy enough without mixing other undertakings with it. Since God gives us leisure to make arrangements for moving out, let us make them; let us pack our bags; let us take an early leave of the company; let us break free from the violent clutches that engage us elsewhere and draw us away from ourselves. We must untie these bonds that are so powerful, and henceforth love this and that, but be wedded only to ourselves. That is to say, let the other things be ours, but not joined and glued to us so strongly that they cannot be detached without tearing off our skin and some part of our flesh as well. The greatest thing in the world is to know how to belong to oneself. It is time to untie ourselves from society, since we can contribute nothing to it. And he who cannot lend, let him keep from borrowing. Our powers are failing us; let us withdraw them and concentrate them on ourselves. He who can turn the offices of friendship and fellowship around and fuse them into himself, let him do so. In this decline, which makes him useless, burdensome, and troublesome to others, let him keep from being troublesome to himself, and burdensome, and useless. Let him indulge and care for himself, and especially govern himself, respecting and fearing his reason and his conscience, so that he cannot make a false step in their presence without shame. *For it is rare for anyone to respect himself enough* [Quintilian].

Socrates says that the young should get instruction; that grown men should practice doing good; and that old men should withdraw from all civil and military occupations and live at their own discretion, without being tied down to any fixed office. There are some temperaments more suited to these precepts for retirement than others. Those whose susceptibility is weak and lax, and whose affection and will are fastidious and slow to enter service or employment—of whom I am one, both by natural disposition and by conviction—will comply with this advice better than will the active and busy souls who embrace everything and engage themselves everywhere, who grow passionate about all things, who offer, present, and give themselves on all occasions.

We should use these accidental and external conveniences, so far as they are agreeable to us, but without making them our mainstay; they are not; neither reason nor nature will have it so. Why should we, contrary to their laws, enslave our contentment to the power of others? Moreover, to anticipate the accidents of fortune; to deprive ourselves of the commodities that are in our hands, as many have done through piety and some philosophers through reason; to wait on ourselves; to sleep on the hard ground; to put out our eyes; to throw our riches into the river; to seek pain, some in order to win bliss in another life by torment in this, others to make themselves safe from a new fall by settling on the lowest step–these are the acts of an excessive virtue. Let the sturdier and stronger natures make even their hiding place glorious and exemplary:

When riches fail, I praise
The safe and simple life, content with
humble ways; But then, when better, richer
fortune smiles on me, I say that only they
live well and sensibly whose wealth in
country manors glistens brilliantly. (Horace)

I have enough on my hands without going that far. It is enough for me while under fortune's favor, to prepare for its disfavor, and while I am well off, to picture the evil that is to come, as far as my imagination can reach; just as we accustom ourselves to jousts and tournaments, and imitate war in the midst of peace.

I do not consider the philosopher Arcesilaus less virtuous because I know that he used gold and silver vessels as much as his fortune allowed him to; and I esteem him more highly for having used them moderately and liberally than if he had given them up.

I see to what limits natural necessity goes; and, thinking about the poor beggar at my door, often merrier and healthier than myself, I put myself in his place, I try to ft my mind to his bias. And running over the other examples in the same way, though I may think that death, poverty, contempt, and disease are at my heels, I easily resolve not to take fright at what a lesser man than I accepts with such patience. I cannot believe that meanness of understanding can do more than vigor, or that the effects of reason cannot match the effects of habit. And knowing how precarious these incidental comforts are, I do not fail, while in full enjoyment of them, to make it my sovereign request of God that he make me content with myself and the good things I bring forth. I see hearty young men who never fail to carry in their baggage a mass of pills to take when afflicted with a cold, which they fear the less because they think they have the remedy at hand. Thus we must do; and further, if we feel ourselves subject to some graver malady, we must provide ourselves with the drugs that benumb and put to sleep the affected part.

The occupation we must choose for such a life must be neither laborious nor annoying; otherwise there would be no point in having come to it in search of rest. This depends on each man's particular taste: mine is not at all adaptable to household management. Those who like it should apply themselves to it with moderation:

Try to bend things to them, not them to things.
(Horace)

Besides, the care of an estate is a job for slaves, as Sallust calls it. Some parts of it are more excusable, like the care of gardens, which Xenophon attributes to Cyrus; and a mean may be found between that base and sordid concern, tense and full of anxiety, which is seen in men who plunge themselves deep into it, and that profound and extreme negligence, letting everything go to seed, which we see in others:

Democritus' herds devour his season's yield,
While his swift soul without his body roams
afield. (Horace)

But let us hear the counsel that the younger Pliny gives his friend Cornelius Rufus on this matter of solitude: "I advise you, in this full and prosperous retreat of yours, to leave to your servants the sordid and abject care of the household, and to devote yourself to the study of letters, in order to derive from them something that is all your own." He means reputation, being of a like temper with Cicero, who says he wants to use his solitude and rest from public affairs to gain by his writings immortal life:

Is knowledge naught to you unless another
knows that you know all you do? (Persius)

It seems reasonable, when a man talks of retiring from the world, that he should set his gaze outside of it. These men do so only halfway. They indeed arrange their afairs for thetimnewhen they will no longer be there; but by a ridiculous contradiction they still aspire to reap the fruit of their plan from the world when they have left it.

The idea of those who seek solitude for religious reasons, filling their hearts with the certainty of divine promises for the other life, is much more sane and consistent. They set before their eyes God, an object infinite both in goodness and in power; in him the soul has the wherewithal to satisfy its desires abundantly in complete freedom. Afflictions, sufferings, come to them as profit, being used for the acquisition of eternal health and rejoicing; death is to be desired, being the passage to so perfect a state. The harshness of their rules is promptly smoothed by habit; and the carnal appetites are frustrated and then put to sleep by denial, for nothing keeps them up but use and exercise. Only this one goal of another life, happily immortal, rightly deserves that we abandon the comforts and pleasures of this life of ours. And he who can really and constantly kindle his soul with the flame of that living faith and hope, builds himself in solitude a life that is voluptuous and delightful beyond any other kind of life.

Therefore I am satisfied with neither the purpose nor the means of Pliny's advice; we still would merely fall out of an ague into a burning fever. This occupation with books is as laborious as any other, and as much an enemy to health, which should be our chief consideration. And we must not let ourselves be lulled to sleep by the pleasure we take in it; it is the same pleasure that ruins the frugal man, the miser, the voluptuous man, and the ambitious man. The sages teach us often enough to beware of the treachery of our appetites, and to distinguish true and entire pleasures from pleasures that are mixed and streaked with a preponderance of pain.

For most pleasures, they say, caress and embrace us only to strangle us, like those thieves that the Egyptians called Philistas. If we got our headache before getting drunk, we should take care not to drink too much; but pleasure, to deceive us, walks ahead and hides her sequel from us. Books are pleasant; but if by associating with them we end by losing gaiety and health, the best parts of us, let us leave them. I am one of those who think that their benefits cannot counterbalance this loss.

As men who have long felt weakened by some indisposition at last give themselves up to the mercy of medicine and have certain rules of living prescribed for them by art, rules which are nevermore to be transgressed; so he who retires, annoyed and disgusted with the common way of life, must model his new life on the rules of reason, order it and arrange it by premeditation and reflection. He must have taken leave of every kind of labor, whatever aspect it may bear; he must lee in general the passions that prevent tranquillity of body and soul, and choose the way that suits his humor best:

Let each one know the way that he should go. (Propertius)

In household management, in study, in hunting, and in all other pursuits, we should take part up to the utmost limits of pleasure, but beware of engaging ourselves further, where it begins to be mingled with pain. We must reserve only so much business and occupation as we need to keep us in trim and protect ourselves from the inconveniences that the other extreme, slack and sluggish idleness, brings in its train.

There are sterile and thorny sciences, for the most part created for the busy life; we must leave them to those who are in the service of the world. For myself, I like only pleasant and easy books, which entertain me, or those that console me and counsel me to regulate my life and my death:

To saunter silent through the wholesome wood, bent on thoughts worthy of the wise and good. (Horace)

Wiser men, having a strong and vigorous soul, can make for themselves a wholly spiritual repose. But I, who have a commonplace soul, must help support myself by bodily comforts; and since age has lately robbed me of those that were more to my fancy, I train and sharpen my appetite for those that remain and are more suitable to this present season. We must hold on, tooth and nail, to our enjoyment of the pleasures of life, which our years tear, one after the other, from our hands:

Let us seize pleasures; life is ours to claim;
Too soon we shall be ashes, ghosts, a name.
(Persius)

Now, as for glory, the goal that Pliny and Cicero set up for us, it is very far from my reckoning. The humor most directly opposite to retirement is ambition. Glory and repose are things that cannot lodge in the same dwelling. As far as I can see, these men have only their arms and legs outside the crowd; their souls, their intentions, are more than ever in the thick of it:

Old man, do you cull scraps for others' ears?
(Persius)

They have only stepped back to make a better jump, to get a stronger impetus wherewith to plunge deeper into the crowd. Do you want to see how they shoot a grain's length too short? Let us put into the scales the advice of two philosophers (Epicurus and Seneca) of two very different sects, one writing to Idomeneus, the other to Lucilius, their friends, to persuade them to give up handling affairs and withdraw from their high positions into solitude.

"You have," they say, "lived until now swimming and floating; come away and die in port. You have given the rest of your life to light; give this part to the shade. It is impossible to abandon occupations if you do not abandon the fruits of them; therefore rid yourself of all care for reputation and glory. There is danger that the gleam of your past actions may give you only too much light and follow you right into your lair. Abandon with the other pleasures that which comes from the approbation of others; and as for your knowledge and ability, don't worry, it will not lose its effect if it makes you yourself a better man.

Remember the man who, when asked why he took so much pains in an art which could come to the knowledge of so few people, replied: Few are enough for me, one is enough for me, none at all is enough for me. He spoke truly: you and one companion are an adequate theater for each other, or you for yourself. Let the people be one to you, and let one be a whole people to you. It is a base ambition to want to derive glory from our idleness and our concealment. We must do like the animals that rub out their tracks at the entrance to their lairs.

"Seek no longer that the world should speak of you, but how you should speak to yourself. Retire into yourself, but first prepare to receive yourself there; it would be madness to trust in yourself if you do not know how to govern yourself. There are ways to fail in solitude as well as in company. Until you have made yourself such that you dare not trip up in your own presence, and until you feel both shame and respect for yourself, *let true ideals be kept before your mind* (Cicero), keep ever in your mind Cato, Phocion, and Aristides, in whose presence even fools would hide their faults; make them controllers of all your intentions; if these intentions get off the track, your reverence for those men will set them right again. They will keep you in a fair way to be content with yourself, to borrow nothing except from yourself, to arrest your mind and fix it on definite and limited thoughts in which it may take pleasure; and, after understanding the true blessings, which we enjoy in so far as we understand them, to rest content with them, without any desire to prolong life and reputation."

That is the counsel of true and natural philosophy, not of an ostentatious and talky philosophy like that of Pliny and Cicero.

Castles from the Air
by **William Douglas Simpson**
1949

William Douglas Simpson (1896-1968) was a Scottish academic and writer who focused on the study of medieval architecture and archeology. Although he was not a trained archeologist, he wrote numerous books and papers based on the excavations he directed at several castles, such as Kildrummy, Kindrochit, Esslemont, Dundarg or Finavon Castle. While he became a well-known authority on the castellated architecture of Scotland and Scandinavia, his detailed studies of castles and its remaining structures are key documents even today. He published the books Dundarg Castle (1954) Scottish Castles: An introduction to the Castles of Scotland (1959) and The Highlands of Scotland (1976), among others. This text was published as the introduction in this famous book Castles from the Air (1949), which it is thought to have amplified Louis Kahn's passion for British castles.

Original Text: Introduction, by William D. Simpson, from Simpson, William Douglas. Castles from the Air. London: Country Life, 1949, pp. 9-16.

The castles of England appeal to every one of us. Their picturesqueness of aspect, whether still occupied or in time-worn ruins; the beautiful scenery amidst which so many of them are found; the striking situations so often chosen for security; the image which they call up to our minds of a society so different from ours; the great historical events of which many of them have been the scene–all these things combine to make our ancient castles a part of our national heritage which is more and more appreciated by the traveling public. In these distressful times it seems probable that facilities for Continental travel will continue to be much restricted, so that more and more of our people will be compelled to extend their acquaintanceship with the glories of our English countryside. At a time when popular interest in our old 'castles is thus likely to increase, air photography reveals them to us in a new aspect. The whole ordaining of the building, the devising and balance of its masses, the way in which it is fitted to its site, the articulation of masonry, earthwork and water defenses, the happy marriage between mansion and gardens, the whole way in which a great house, or a shattered ruin, sits into its surroundings-all these can now be studied from an angle, at once physical and mental, not hitherto available. To introduce to English readers our castles from the air is the purpose of this book.

Most people take a grim view of our castles. "Like the seer in the Odyssey," it has been said, "they see their walls dripping with blood." Those dark vaults below, which in plain fact were built for the storage of food in days when a great house had to be self-supporting–when there was no tradesman's van to call with the daily order–become, in the popular fancy, ghastly dungeons in which captives pined, or underwent torments unspeakable. Those mural closets, designed for purely domestic purposes, are transformed into secret chambers wherein dark plots were hatched, or hideouts when once the foe had gained the gates. And the castle as a whole is regarded far too much from a purely military standpoint. It is pictured as resounding, day and night, to the tramp and clash of mail-clad men, ever ready for instant combat:

They quitted not their harness bright,
Neither by day, nor yet by night:
They lay down to rest,
With corset laced,
Pillowed on buckler cold and hard:
They carved at the meal,
With gloves of steel,
And they drank the red wine through the
helmet barred.

In sober fact, the medieval castle was first and foremost a country gentleman's seat, upon which the needs of a scrambling and unquiet time imposed a fortified carapace. It was not normally armed to the teeth, or stuffed with a garrison of professional soldiers, each at his action station. In time of peace, it would simply contain the lord's familia or household; in his frequent absences no more than a caretaker and a servant or two. In time of war the castle would be garrisoned by the lord's tenantry who dwelt around, and who would be called up for their service under the feudal obligation known as "castle-guard."

It is, indeed, as a local centre of feudalism that the castle of the Middle Ages differs essentially, both from a modern country house and from the military works of the Roman Empire or of a modern state. Our fortifications to-day are public concerns, built, maintained, and garrisoned by the central government. Such, also, were the military works of the Roman Empire; for example, the forts which were built on the "Saxon Shore" for the defense of Britain against overseas invaders. The medieval castle, on the other hand, was a military work built, maintained, and garrisoned on behalf of the government by a private landlord. Again, the relations of a modern landlord with his tenantry, sentiment apart, are purely economic–the paying of rent on the one hand and the receiving of it on the other, with the respective statutory obligations attached thereto. But the feudal landlord, in addition to exacting rents from his tenantry, was charged with the powers of local government over them. In his barony court he judged them, like in civil and in criminal cases; in the castle pit he imprisoned those condemned, and on his gibbet, he strung them up. In time of war the tenantry gathered in the castle court and marched out under their lord's banner to join the national army. Such, in rough essence, was feudalism–a system in which ownership of land was burdened with the responsibility for local government and local defense.

Despite much that has been written by modern propagandists, this feudal system was by no means wholly, or even mainly, the result of a wicked usurpation by the big man of tyrannical powers over the small men. It arose inevitably out of the breakdown of public order in Western Europe at the fall of the Roman Empire. The highly trained Roman legions were no longer there to maintain the fabric of public order. The great Roman roads, with their admirable posting system which enabled the imperial government to execute its behests from Newcastle to Palmyra, from Vienna on the Danube to Thebes upon the Nile, had fallen into decay. Amid the general collapse of security, the populations of the Roman provinces now falling asunder were forced to organize themselves for their own government and defense. Inevitably this took place under the leadership of the big men on the spot–the landlords.

Stepping in where the central government had withdrawn, the Gaulish landlords organized their tenants, provided them with arms, trained them to use these, decided disputes among them and administered justice in manorial courts. Into this nascent feudalism the Franks and Goths, pouring in across the frontiers now abandoned by the legions, injected the Nordic ideals of chivalry, of the faith due by vassal to suzerain and by suzerain to vassal. The Christian Church, preserving what was left of the old Roman law and order, imposed upon the system a legal framework, and invested it with a religious sanction. Such was feudalism. Its outward and visible sign was the fortified residence of the Frankish overlord, superseding the undefended villa of his Gallo-Roman predecessor.

Of course, the new system had its evil side. Its great curse was a private war between rival magnates. It was under the impulse of private war that the feudal castle developed in western Europe. Many centuries would pass here the modern states, resuming the responsibilities which the Roman Empire had abdicated, would impose law and order upon their lieges on their own account, instead of through the feudal magnate. When that day came the feudal castle had outlived its purpose. Its work was done, and it sank into ruins, or was transformed into a stately country house. Whether in the one condition or in the other, it survives as a symbol of a stage through which every western European state has had to pass; as the memorial of a system that was the nursery of our institutions, local and national, and has left abiding traces upon British life.

The feudal system, in its fully developed form, was introduced into this country by the Norman conquerors. Wherever a Norman baron settled himself down, there he threw up a castle as a fortified residence in which he could maintain himself against his rivals and the Saxon peasantry. Beside the castle, in course of time, he would build a chapel for the convenience of his household and the tenants who huddled for protection under the skirts of the castle ramparts. As often as not the priest serving this chapel would be a younger brother or son or another kinsman of the lord of the manor. In due course the manor would thus come to be a parish, ecclesiastically considered. The castle chapel would grow into the parish church; and church and castle, side by side, would stand for the ecclesiastical and administrative fulcra of the early parochial organization. To the present day that old-time association of manor and parish, castle, and church, so important for the early development of our local institutions, is seen on the face of England in the frequency with which the remains of a Norman castle are found hard by an ancient parish church. Frequent examples of this juxtaposition will be found in the views that follow.

When we think of a Norman castle, we are apt to picture in our mind's eye a great square, buttressed keep like the Tower of London, Rochester Castle or others illustrated in the present volume. Yet the fact is that such stone keeps, particularly in the earliest times, were exceptional. The vast majority of our Norman castles were not made of stone and lime at all, but of earthwork and timber. William, says the Bayeux Tapestry, ordered that a castle should be dug at Hastings; and in the picture we see his pioneers hard at work with their spades, and his carpenters busy on the timber superstructure. Nowadays the woodwork has gone or has been replaced in stone; but the banks and ditches and the great central mound remain. Today they form the grand feature of many famous castles, and the feature by which the layout of the whole structure has, once for all, been determined.

We may see several pictures of these timbered earthwork castles in the Bayeux Tapestry. What happened was this: the ordinary Norman baron, who could not afford the stone castle, or whose manor yielded him no building stone, threw up a tall, conical, fat-topped mound, surrounded by a ditch, out of which its materials were dug. This mound he called a motte. Round its summit he set a palisade of stout tree trunks or fence of hurdle-work or gabions, and within it he erected a wooden tower-house. Attached to the motte, in most cases, was a bailey or courtyard, crescentic or shovels-shaped in outline, enclosed by a palisaded bank and ditch; and within this were set the subsidiary buildings—hall, kitchen, chambers, stables, byre, barns, smithy and the rest, all of wood. The complete example of this kind of structure is known to antiquaries as a "mount-and-bailey" castle. Later on, it became the custom to replace the timber defenses with walls of stone and lime—a "shell" round the summit of the motte, and long sweeps of "curtain" cresting the banks of the bailey. In this way some of our noblest castles have originated. Royal Windsor itself is nothing more than a mount-and-bailey castle on a gigantic scale, in this case with a double bailey. Sometimes, as at Lincoln, there is a double motte.

Such castles of timbered earthwork were by no means to be treated cavalierly. It was not easy for heavily armed men to scale the smooth slopes of the mound and, blown as they were, to climb over its well-defended palisade. Nor could the latter be easily pulled to pieces, or fired; and although the wooden buildings would quickly yield to the flames, they could readily be replaced, while the earthworks themselves could be levelled only at a prodigious cost in labour.

These timber castles must have been highly picturesque structures, with their woodwork all gaily painted, as was the custom in the Middle Ages, before men had lost their sense of colour.

Most of our square stone keeps, the alternative type of castle, date from the latter part of the twelfth century. Henry II was a mighty builder of them. The weakness of such a structure lay in its angles. Here the battering-ram or the miner's pick may work with deadly effect, knocking out the corner stones or undermining the entire angle. This happened in the siege of Rochester Castle by King John. Such keeps were usually defended from the parapet, often by means of overhanging timber galleries. The loopholes in the basement, mere slits in a wall twelve or fifteen feet thick, were for light and air, not for shooting through. It will readily be understood that parapet defense is least effective just at the angles, where at ground-level the greatest danger lies. Hence from about the end of the twelfth century engineers began to experiment with their stone towers. The way in which their minds were working is seen at Rochester, where the corner brought down by John's miners has been rebuilt as a half-cylinder. At Conisborough we have a great cylindrical tower, strengthened by buttresses like those which clasp the angles of the square keeps. From this it is but a step to omit the buttresses altogether and to build the keep as a plain, smooth cylinder, presenting no angles to an assailant. These great cylindrical keeps or donjons are characteristic of the first half of the thirteenth century. Perhaps the finest example may be seen at Pembroke Castle.

At the same time the engineers were exploring the possibilities of the stone curtain walls which now were replacing the timber defenses of the bailey. The Crusades had introduced the military men of western Europe to the massive defensive works of the Byzantine Empire, with their long wall planes protected by frequent towers, round or square. Such towers were loopholed for archery, while the curtains themselves were threaded by galleries also provided with bow-slits. Moreover, the Crusades had also taught the western warriors something of the highly developed art of siegecraft as practiced in the Near East. To resist an attack conducted with such scientific skill, far heavier and better articulated works were required than the walls and towers hitherto built in western Europe. So, in the thirteenth century the military engineers of France and England, besides building their donjons round instead of square, devoted more and more attention to the curtain walls. They made these thicker and loftier, and drew them so as to enclose an ampler area. At intervals around the enceinte they set towers cylindrical or square, arranged mutually to support each other as well as to flank the curtain walls between them. Above all, they took especial care to secure the entrance, which was now recessed between two gate towers, and defended by one or more portcullises and pairs of folding doors, as well as by meurrières or "murder-holes" in the vaulted passage, and by machicolated jutties overhead on the outside wall, in front and rear.

The interior buildings of the castle were also now, in general, made of stone. Instead of being scattered loosely about the courtyard, they were drawn together so as to form a corps de logis, usually placed along the curtain wall which was farthest from the entrance. In the centre of this corps-de logis was the great hall, at its lower end were the kitchen and offices, and at its upper end the lord's "great chamber" and the private apartments. The brewhouse and bakehouse were placed where most convenient. Every large castle contained a chapel, and care is usually taken to secure that this should be, as far as possible, correctly oriented.

As a result of all these developments, the typical castle of the thirteenth century came to consist of a large enclosure, defended by a curtain wall with flanking towers, usually round but still sometimes square. One of these towers was the donjon or keep, the dernier ressort. This is often isolated from the rest of the castle by its own proper ditch, as the early mottes had been. Two other towers flank the entrance. Within the courtyard, as a rule on the side farthest removed from the gateway, were the principal living apartments. The whole is surrounded by a fosse or moat; and sometimes there is a basecourt. The donjon or keep no longer forms the lord's residence, but tends to fall into disuse, unless in time of war. The lord now lives in the dwelling-house within the courtyard; indeed, in some cases the donjon, perched inconveniently, perhaps, on an old Norman motte, was allowed to become ruinous, and sometimes it was deliberately dismantled. Thus, the thirteenth-century castle comes to be essentially a lord's house, consisting of hall, kitchen and chamber, set within a fenced enclosure. And as time went on, the defenses tended more and more to be concentrated at the entrance, so that the dominant place once held in the castle scheme by the donjon now came to be usurped by the gatehouse.

Most of our greater English castles had come into existence by the end of the thirteenth century. Indeed, the majority of them owe their foundation to the century before, when the feudal baronage reached the height of their power, and well-nigh disrupted the State by their incessant feuds with each other and rebellions against the crown. The strong Plantagenet kings reduced the barons to obedience and sought to control, by the issue of licenses, the building of more castles, with which the country was already over-provided.

In Edward I's reign, therefore, the chief new castles erected were royal fortresses, intended to secure the King's conquest of Wales, and so partaking more of the character of national military works than of feudal castles in the normal sense.

Could we look inside one of the greater English castles of about the year 13oo, we should be struck by the combination of magnificence and rudeness which it would exhibit. Furniture was scanty, consisting mainly of wooden tables, benches, stools, chests and beds. The latter, in important rooms, would be richly carved, and draped with costly stuff. On the walls would be hung splendid tapestries from Italy or the Levant, while the floors were strewn with straw or with sweet-smelling herbs. Into this was cast all the refuse of the feast; and as the straw was not too frequently renewed, the floors were apt to get into an unsavory state. Indeed, if we were to enter a medieval castle, our first sensation would probably be experienced by our noses— the more so as the drains were not lushed by water, as they are in modern houses.

The great hall might have a fireplace, often elaborately carved and painted; but in many cases there was only a central open hearth, with a louvre in the roof through which the smoke escaped, more or less— and often, doubtless, more less than more! By this time the windows were coming to be fitted with glass, sometimes in portable frames which could be taken from castle to castle, accompanying the travels of the lord. The usual practice was for the upper half of the window to be glazed, while the lower had shutters which opened for ventilation. Tapestries and carpets were also thus carried about from house to house. In the minor furnishings of the establishment—table utensils and ornaments and the like—and above all in the fitments of the chapel, objects of striking artistic beauty and craftsmanship would be found. We get a remarkable picture of the rich furnishings of a great English castle in the later Middle Ages in the inventory of the belongings of the famous SirJohn Fastolf–the original of Shakespeare's Falstaff–at Caister Castle, where he died in 1459.

The English castle reaches its climax in the "Edwardian" or concentric fortresses erected to secure the conquest of Wales. Of an Edwardian castle, strictly understood, the distinguishing characteristics are: first, the concentric arrangement of its wards; and second, the presence of a "keep-gatehouse." These two features are quite independent in their origin, and they do not always occur together. There are concentric castles like the Tower of London, or Rhuddlan Castle, which do not have a keep-gatehouse. And there are castles, such as Tonbridge, Llanstephan, Dunstanburgh and Bothal, which possess keep-gatehouses but are not concentric.

The idea of the concentric castle was borrowed by western military engineers from Syria and the Levant, where the Crusades had introduced them to the great fortresses of the Byzantine Empire, in which the concentric principle had descended in unbroken continuity from Roman times. The idea of opposing successive wards, or defensive envelopes, to an attacker was no new one, even in the west. It is fully displayed at Château Gaillard, built by Coeur de Lion about 1196-8. But in the true concentric castle the inner envelope is wholly enclosed by the outer, and as the latter is always much lower the two can be in action against an assailant at the same time. In this simultaneous activation of the entire defensive resources of the garrison lay a major part of the special strength of such castles. The Crusading engineers were quick to grasp the fact, and already in the first quarter of the thirteenth century

we have a completely concentric castle in Syria at Le Krak des Chevaliers. The town of Carcassonne, refortified in the latter half of the century, illustrates the arrival of the new concept in the west. In England, the Tower of London, as reorganized by Henry III and Edward I, is a perfect example of a concentric castle.

On the other hand, the keep-gatehouse appears to be a distinctively English invention. In the castles of the earlier part of the thirteenth century, the donjon or keep is usually at the back or remotest corner of the enceinte, as far removed as possible from the point of greatest danger, and its function is that of a dernier ressort, into which the garrison might retire, if they could, should the rest of the castle be taken. By contrast, in the keep-gatehouse the weight and mass of the castle is brought forward and concentrated frontally. The lord's or governor's residence is combined with the gatehouse, in the forefront of the fight, and the commandant has the drawbridge, portcullises and other defenses of the entrance passage under his immediate personal control-an important safeguard at this period, when the feudal lords were relying less and less on their own vassals and more and more on paid retainers whose fidelity was often doubtful.

At Llanstephan and Dunstanburgh the keep-gatehouse was soon given up as a house of entry. Its entrance passage was walled up frontally, and a new entrance was opened in the curtain wall on the flank. The same alteration took place in the Scottish castles of St. Andrews and Macduff's Castle, and in the Irish castles of Rosecrea and Liscarroll. Clearly the combination of a lord's residence with a gatehouse was found to have practical disadvantages.

The interpolation of the drawbridge and portcullis machinery, not to speak of other defensive tackle, into the midst of the principal residential apartments, was decidedly awkward. At Harlech and Carnarvon the portcullis was operated from the chapel! This is ecclesia militans with a vengeance. At Dunstanburgh, Llanstephan, Tonbridge and Carnarvon the difficulty was got round by relegating the hall to the second floor. But this arrangement was obviously inconvenient. The manifest failure of the keep-gatehouse plan to combine the requirements of residence and defense, coupled with the fact that this type of structure emerged so near the end of English castle-building, gives the type a limited chronological range—say from 1270 to 1370. It is no longer found in Bodiam Castle, Sussex, erected pursuant to a license granted in 1385. Its absence there is the more significant because Bodiam is a strong fortress, erected, as the terms of its license show, to subserve national military needs. But if Bodiam has no keep-gatehouse, it displays on the other hand, in remarkable perfection, the characteristic late medieval provision of a separate suite of quarters for the standing garrisons of professional soldiers which were now, under the altered conditions of warfare, maintained in the larger castles.

By this time the days of castle-building in England were virtually over. It is true that the recrudescence of feudal anarchy in the fourteenth and fifteenth centuries, culminating in the Wars of the Roses, led to the erection, in connection with already existing castles, of a number of strong towers of specialized types, like those of Dudley, Warkworth, Tattershall, Raglan and Ashby-de-la-Zouch. But these are exceptional phenomena, and do not affect the broad generalisation that by this time the castle has yielded pride of place to the manor-house.

Yet in the north of England, behind the Scottish Border, where warlike conditions persisted for another two hundred years, the old Norman tradition of a square keep or tower-house was never forgotten, and throughout the fourteenth and fifteenth centuries we find numerous baron's houses, some of them large, some of them small, built on this plan. These northern tower-houses are not the great crown fortresses or the strongholds of mighty feudal lords. They are the residences of the intermediate and minor landowners; and the significant point about them is that they are entirely different in kind from the sort of dwelling in which these lesser gentry had been living before the Plantagenet attack upon Scotland. Before that unhappy venture the country squires had dwelt in timber or stone-built halls, having at the upper end the camera or private room, and at the lower end the kitchen and offices. We can study at Aydon Castle how such a peaceful establishment, in those iron years of war, had to be enclosed with a fortified wall; and we have its builder's own word for it, in 1315s, that "he had lately fortified his dwelling house at Ayden with a wall of stone and lime against the King's enemies, the Scots." Where a house was being erected de novo, it had perforce, under the new conditions, to be designed as a strong fortalice. For such requirements, in the case of a landowner of moderate resources, the scheme of a simple rectangular tower was obviously alike the most defensible and the most convenient. Such tower-houses are simply the current layout of the hall-house, up-ended for security reasons. They contain the normal sequence of kitchen, hall, great chamber and bedrooms, only these are now piled on top of each other for purposes of defense.

The stern reality of the castle disappeared once the strong Tudor monarchs had put an end to the feudal power and private armies of the baronage. But the prestige of the name survived, and it was still applied to some of the great unfortified country houses of Elizabethan times–just as the outward trappings of the castle, in the form of round or square towers, mock battlements and even moats, continued to be used in some of the architectural designs of that period. But the end of the tale had yet to come. A second innings was offered to our English castles by the Civil War of the seventeenth century. Their stout old walls, organized for artillery defense, and sometimes, as at Donnington, blanketed by earthworks, were able to offer a prolonged resistance to the Parliamentary cannon. Held mostly in the royal cause, the castles of England thus literally went down fighting, and made a last stand that crowned them with honour, By the Parliament they were "slighted," and the devastation wrought by Puritan gunpowder may still be seen in many a shattered ruin. In not a few cases such a fate may be thought to have added to their charm:

Time has mouldered into beauty many a tower,
Which, when it frowned with all its battlements,
Was only terrible.

Architectural
Precedents
Historic Case Studies
on Spatial Density and
Seclusion

British Castles

53.339960, -1.777516

**Peveril Castle
Castleton, England**

Peveril Castle, located in the English countryside of Derbyshire, overlooks the village of Castleton dominating from the hilltop. Its square plan is roughly 40 feet, with walls 8 feet thick. This now ruined castle is formerly known as Peak castle, originally named after the cavern it rests upon, and was built by the feudal baron, William Peveril. Constructed with stone in a distinct herringbone masonry pattern, rather than the timber that was typically used for Norman castles during this period.

Its intricate square plan has its programmatic extremities encompassing the central uniform rectangular atrium. An overarching carving from this dense stone atop the hillside is indicative of the opening to the world that is being represented in section. The thick outer shell protects and nourishes the open space in the interior central core. With apertures breaking the boundary to allow for moments of natural light which instill a sense of hope. This crenellated tower serves as a testament to power and fortitude.

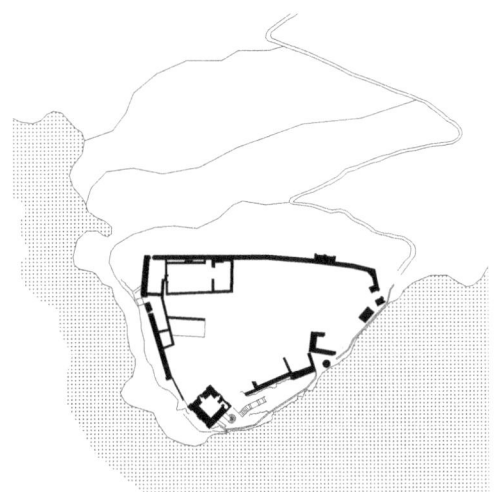

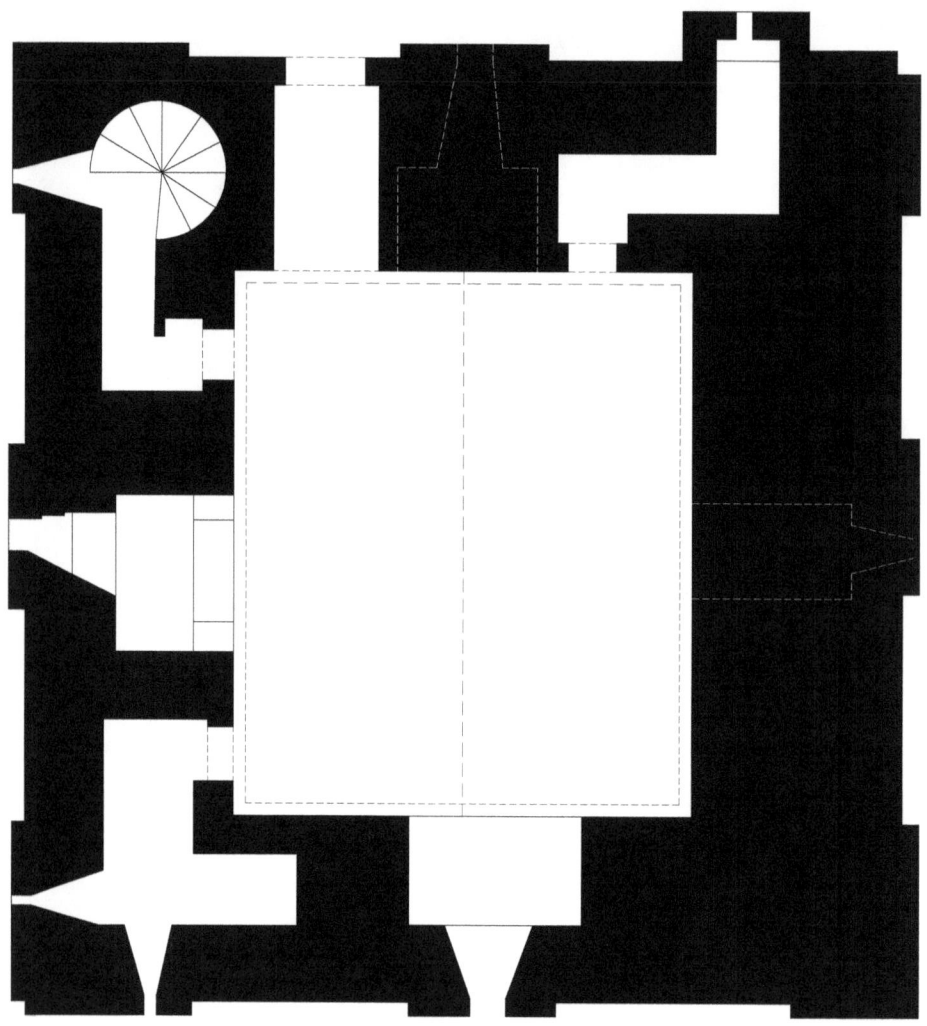

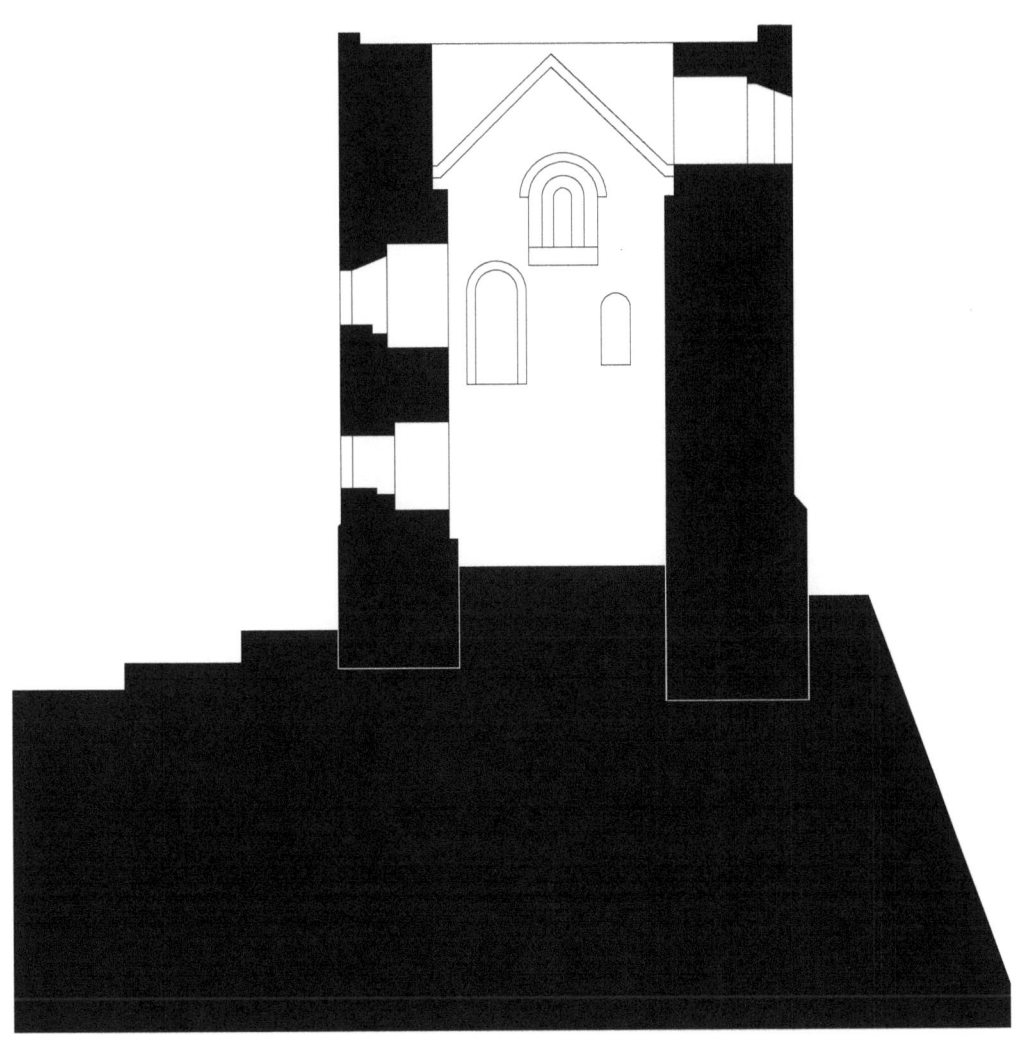

Peveril Castle, Castleton, England

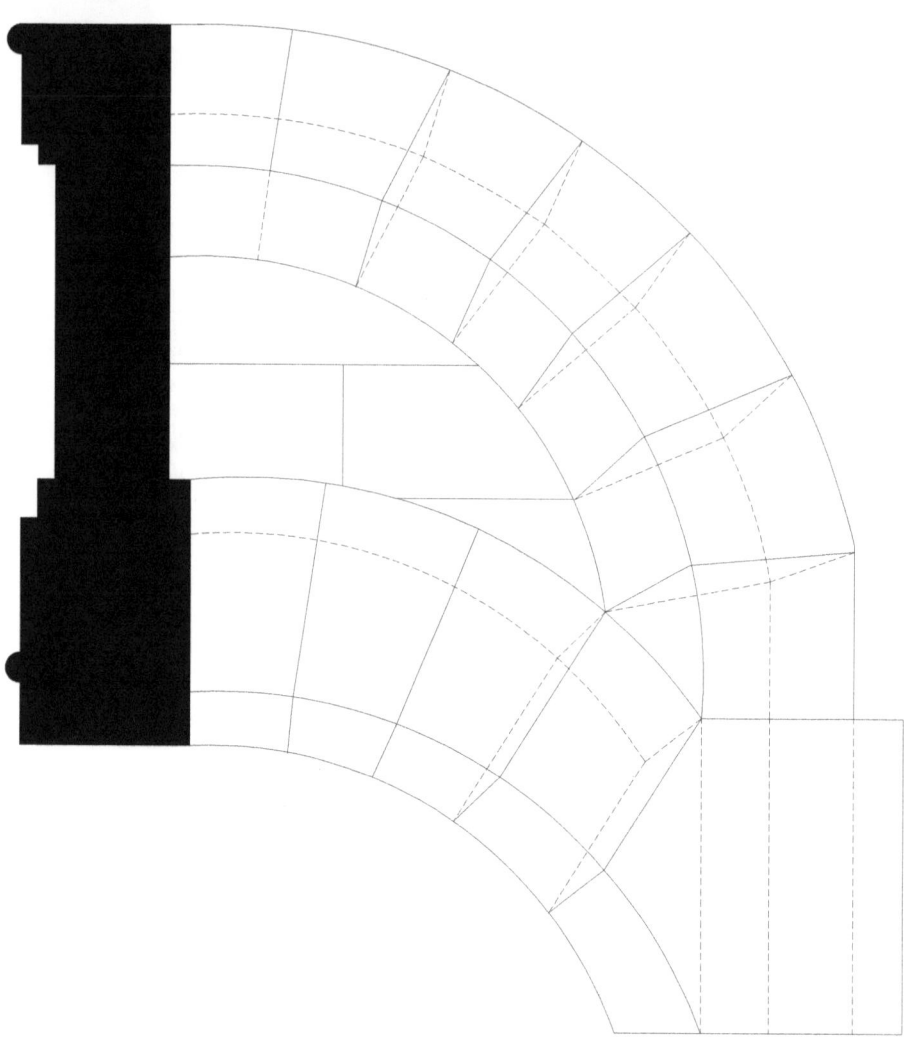

Architectural Precedents | Historic Case Studies

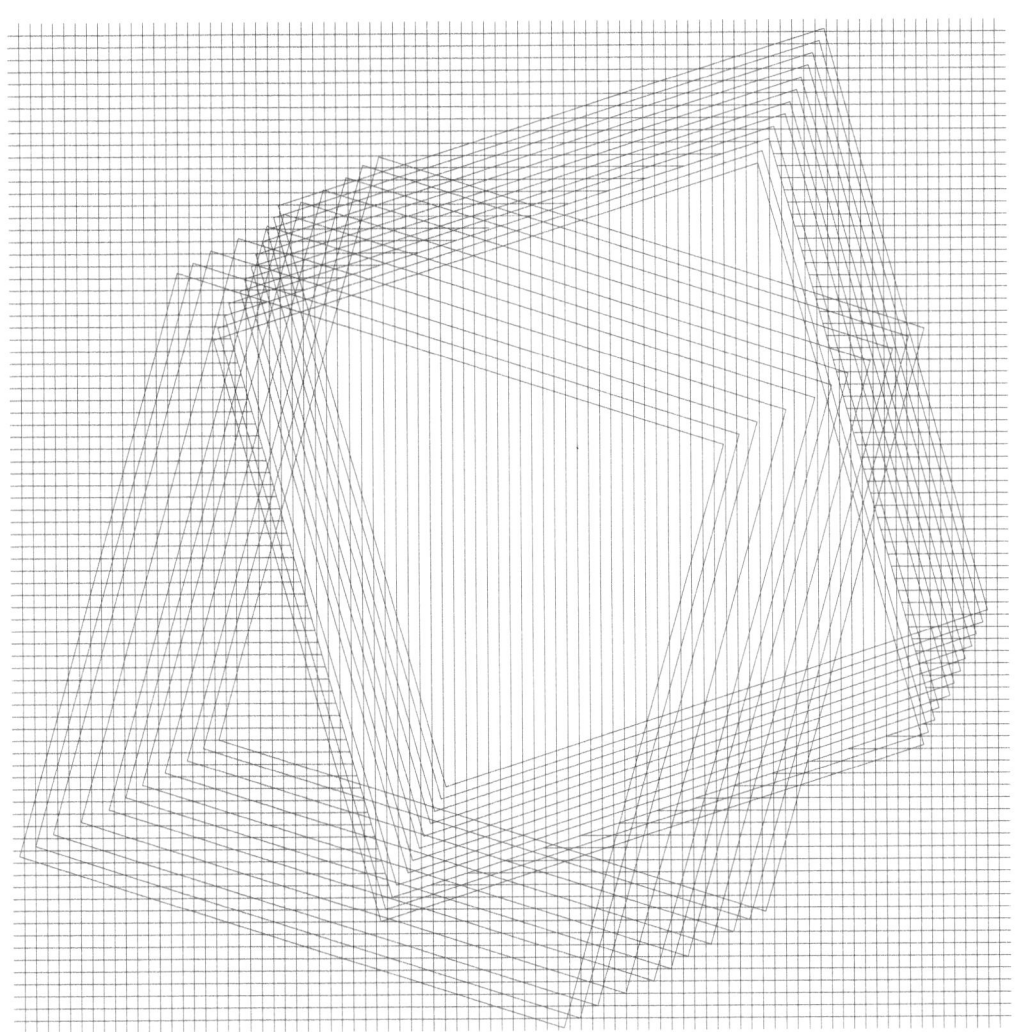

Peveril Castle, Castleton, England

51.129593, 1.321283

Dover castle, located in Dover, Kent, began its fortification in the 12th century by King Henry II. Strategically placed on the edge of England, this castle stands as the first line of defense. As a response to the constant demands of warfare the enclosure continued to grow for hundreds of years. Including a series of tunnels that were placed throughout the Napoleonic war. The relevance of this motte and bailey structure has been extended with the addition of barracks and an adaptation to modern warfare.

 This complex fortress palimpsest of fortification withstands the test of time. Stemming from the central dual rectangular core are a series of peculiar programmatic extremities. Rooted in the facade are miniscule apertures that open up to the interior allowing for a protection of natural light. A seemingly impenetrable stronghold has proven to be able to withstand and shield. This goliath of a castle has been defended through shear massing and manipulation of the environment.

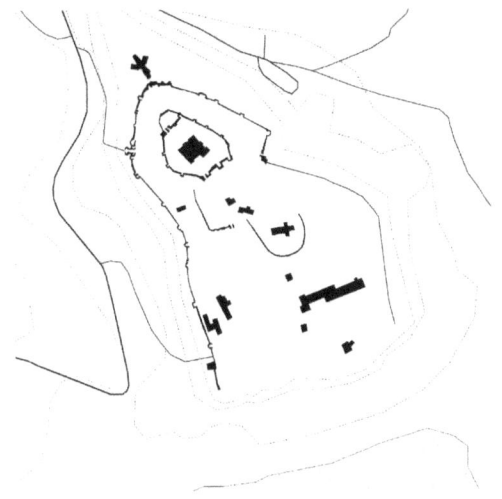
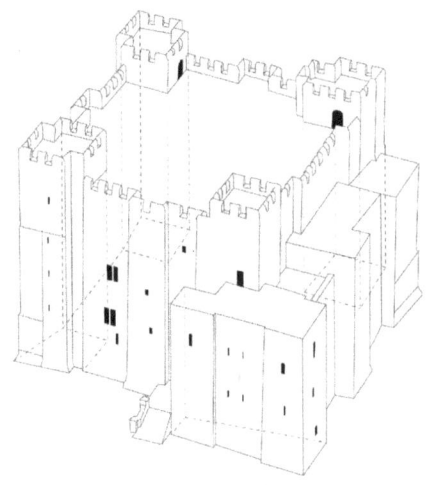

Dover Castle, Kent, England

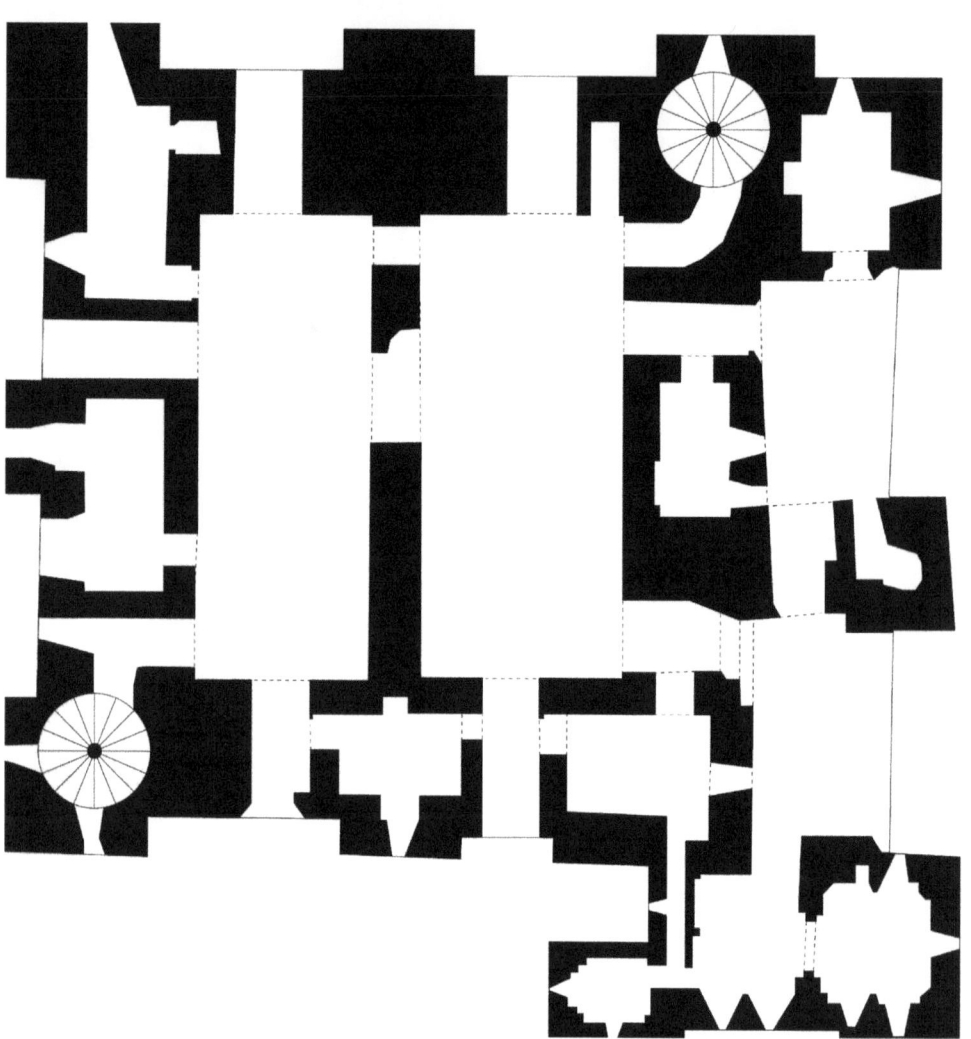

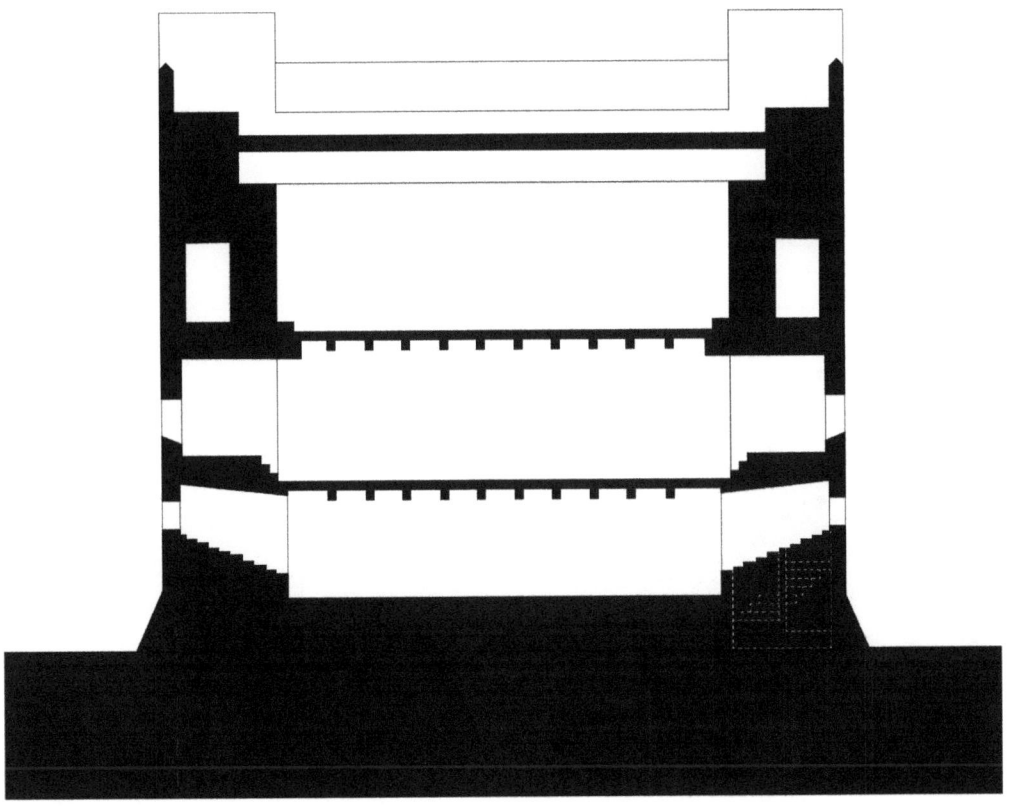

Dover Castle, Kent, England

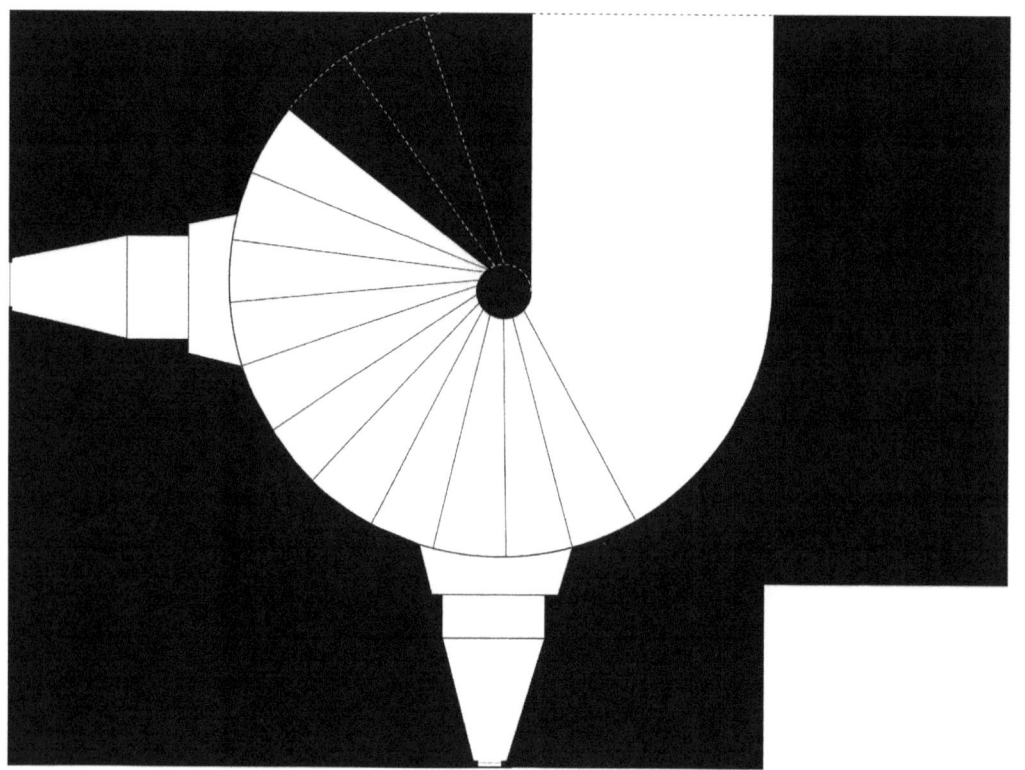

Dover Castle, Kent, England

Hedingham Castle
Essex, England

Hedingham Castle, located in the village of Castle Hedingham, traces its roots to the late 11th and early 12th century. Standing to a height of 110 feet, with 10 to 11 feet thick walls. Initially a motte-and-bailey structure, it evolved into a formidable stone keep surrounded by concentric defensive walls. The stronghold belonged to the influential de Vere family for centuries, witnessing key historical events. It succumbed to King John in the early years of 1216 c.e. during the First Barons' War.

The dense symmetry of the castle instills a deep sense of protection, further fortified by its seclusion. With the concentric walls depicting a layered defense, each contributing to an intricate whole. Ornate moments in the plans and window pattern attempt to break through from this symmetry in order to deal with programmatic qualities. Two towers each placed on an opposite diagonal corner of the castle served as battlements. Its formal rectilinear cuboid presence emphasizes solidity and permanence.

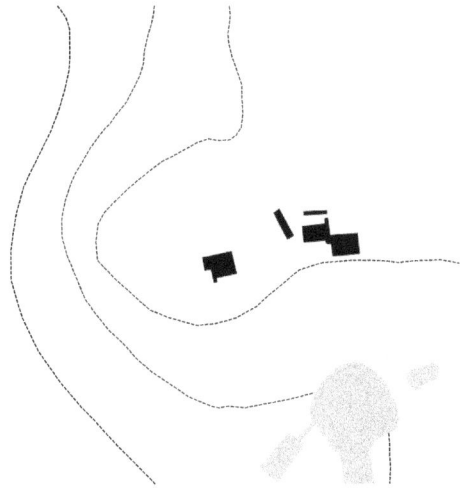
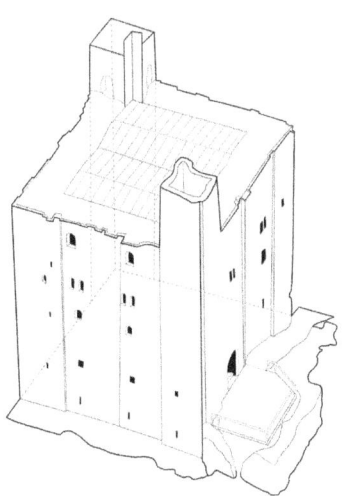

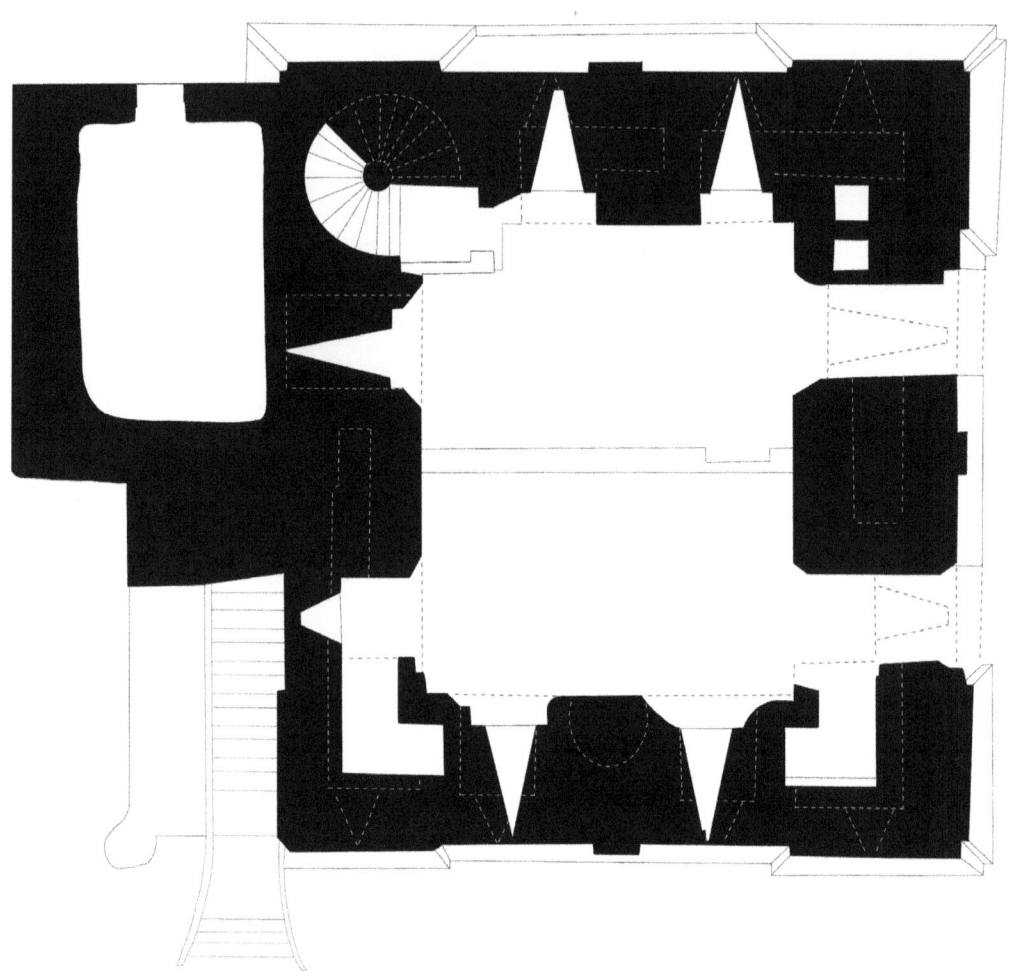

Hedingham Castle, Essex, England

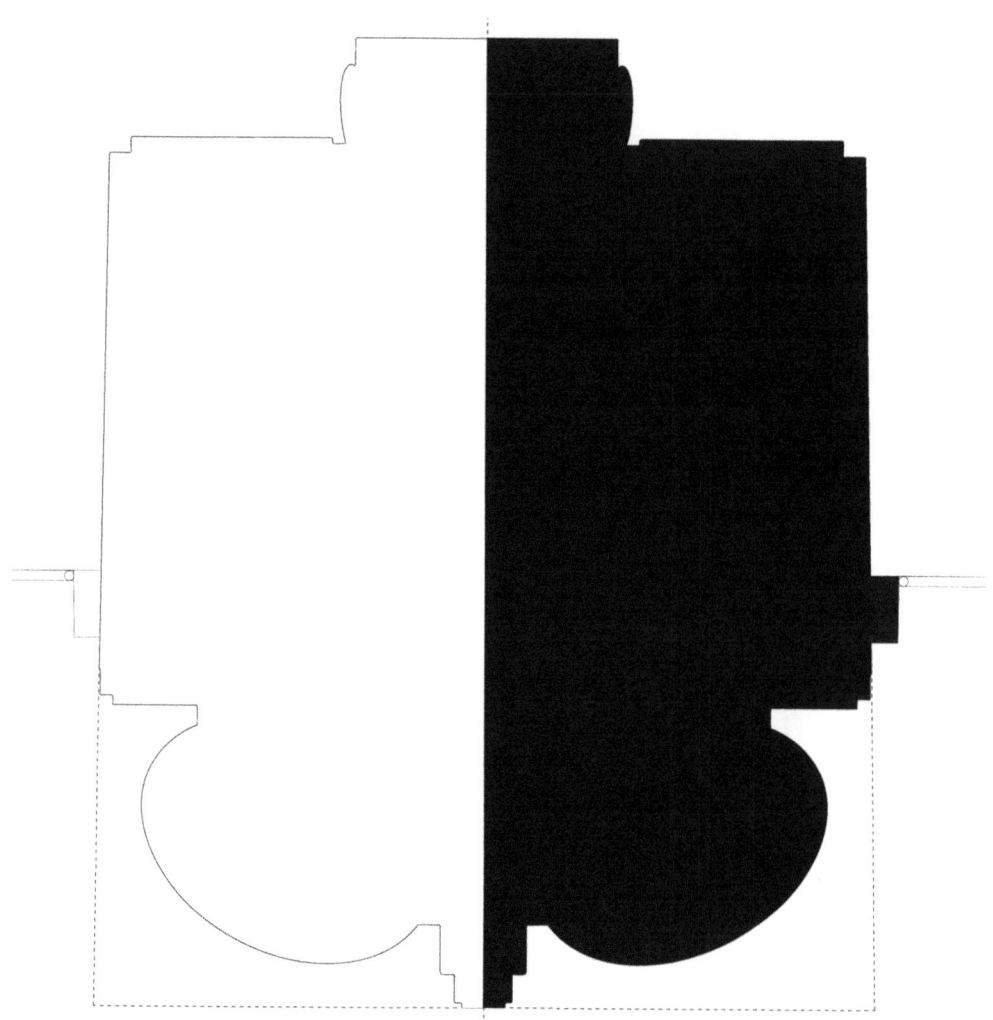

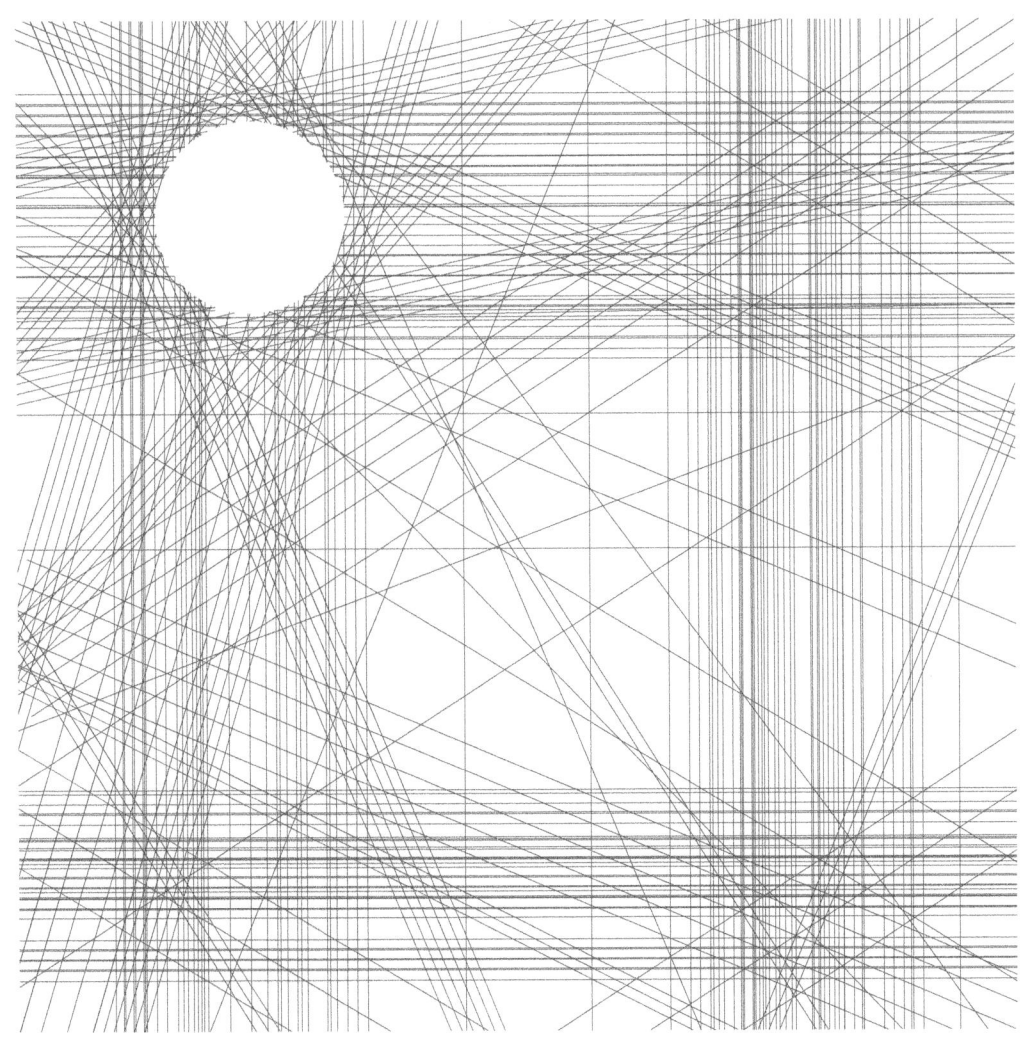

52.094279, 1.530769

Orford Castle
Suffolk, England

Orford Castle, located in the English county of Suffolk, and was built in the 12th century by King Henry II of England. Designed to withstand the dominating power of East Anglian Barons, as a way to guard the royal family. The castle was able to bring together the royal power of the region in support. Originally standing at a grand 90 feet, this keep and bailey castle was constructed surrounded by curtain walls and varying mounds. It eventually became the residence for several feudal lords.

The mostly preserved keep is a testament to this monolithic stone structure's defensive capabilities. Emanating from the rounded central core is a triangular configuration of towers that brings together a tight amalgamation of density in the massing. Minute moments of natural light are perforating the castle to bring life into the otherwise solid voids on the outer shell. The three towers serve as a guise that hides the open circular atrium, allowing it to safely connect with the world.

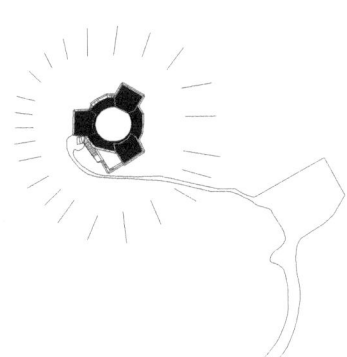

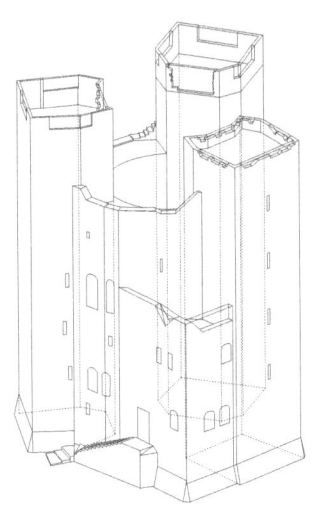

Orford Castle, Suffolk, England

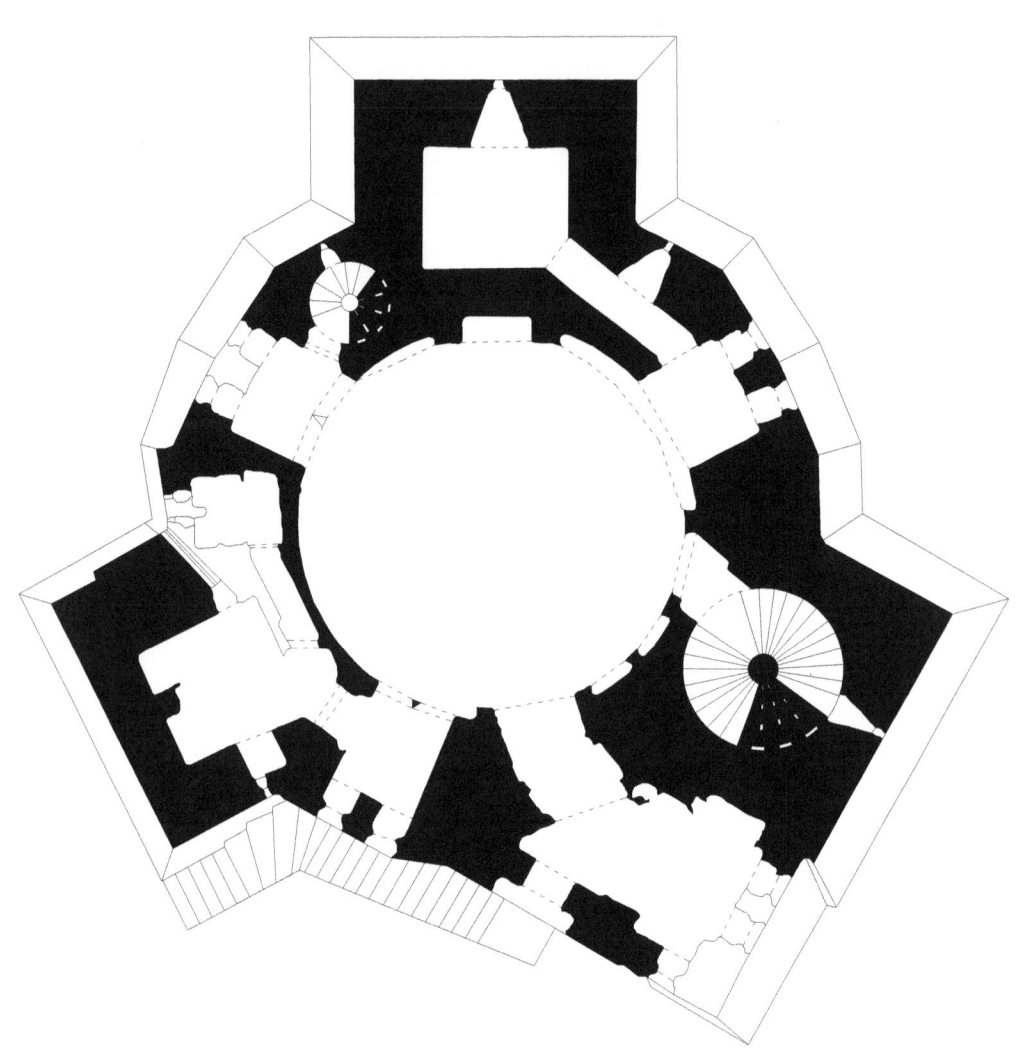

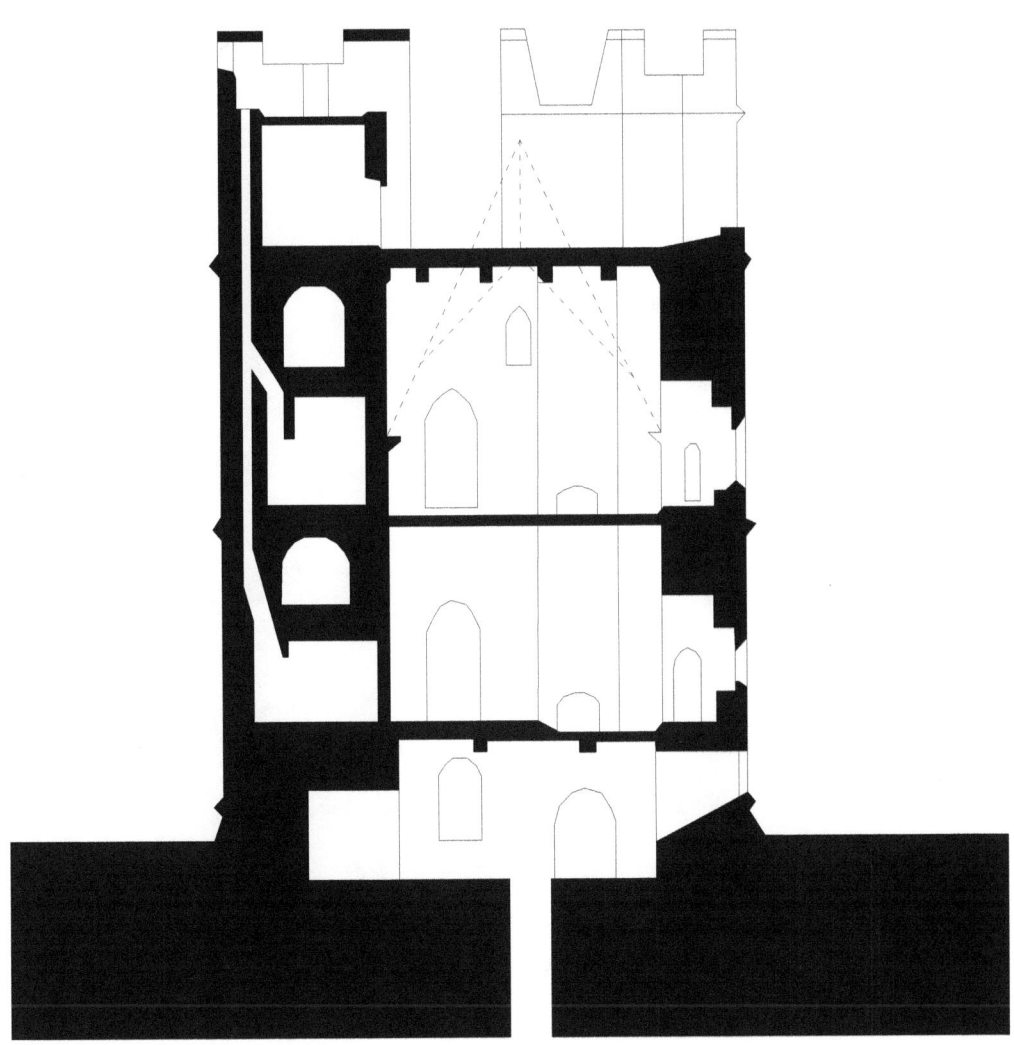

Orford Castle, Suffolk, England   51

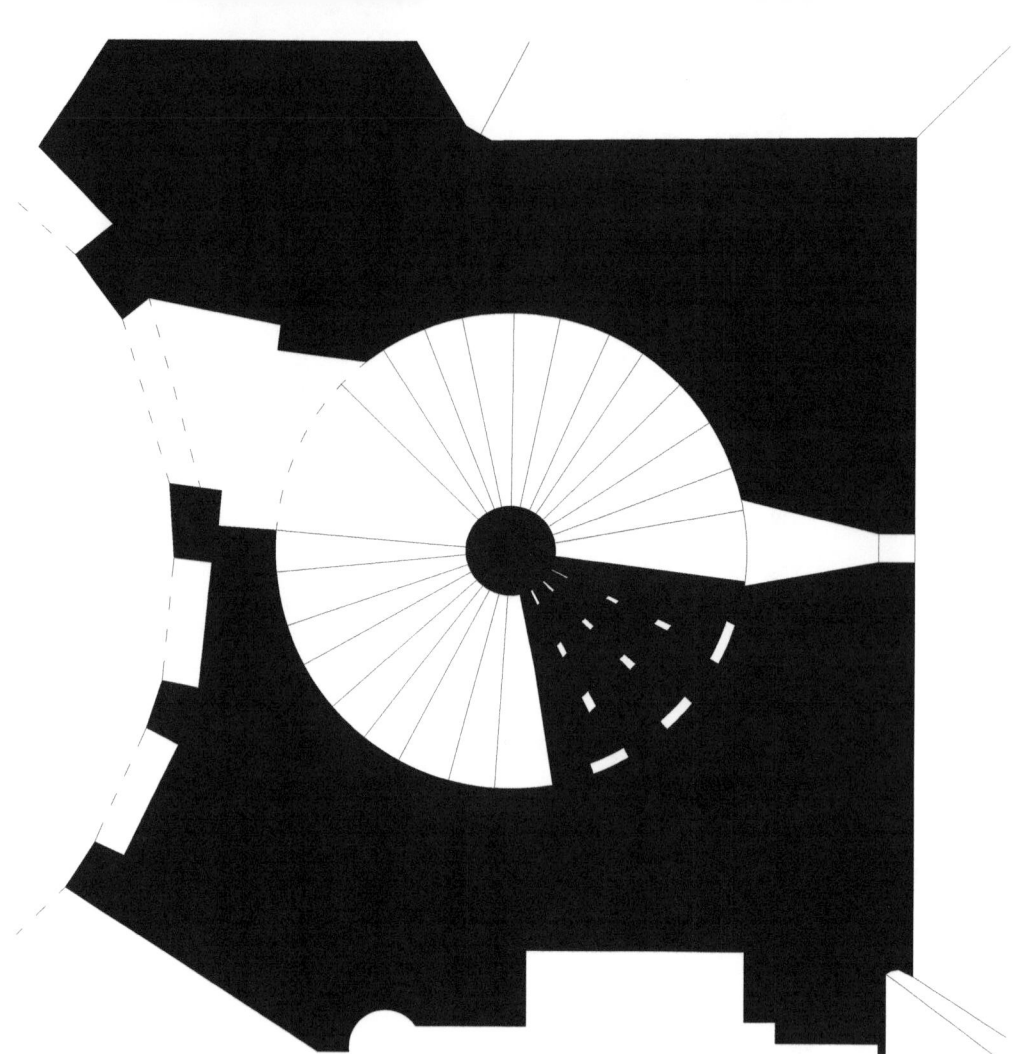

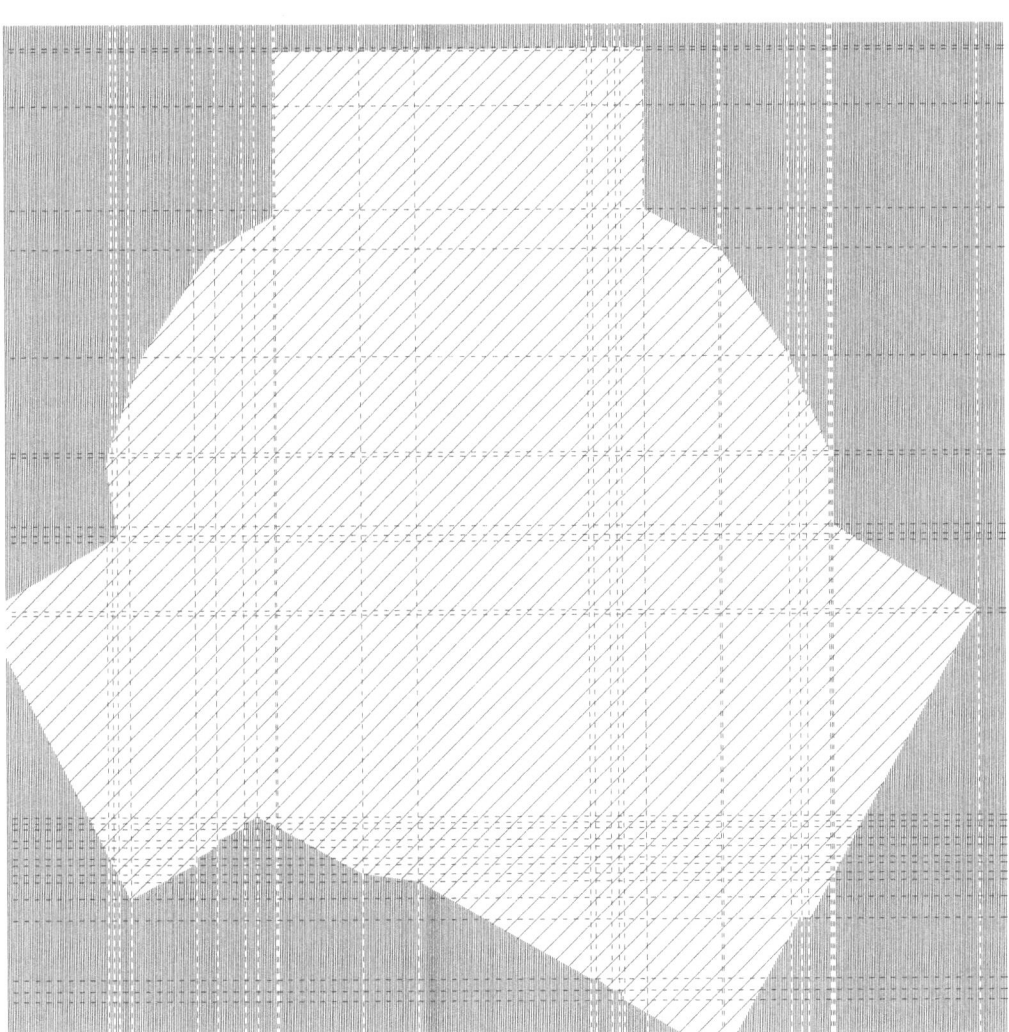

Orford Castle, Suffolk, England

53.554321, -6.789738

Trim castle, located south of the Riven
Boyne in Trim County Meath, was built
by the de Lacy family in the 12th century.
A symmetrically balanced massing built
shortly after the arrival of the Anglo-Normans
in Ireland. Location was determined by
a landscape that would ensure a natural
seclusion. A three story keep served as a
stronghold to a baron who was fighting for
control over his newly appointed land. This
castle stood at 75 feet tall with 11 feet thick
walls.

A cruciform massing and composition
is being brought into this building to show a
sense of hierarchy from the outside world.
Four towers surround the central tower,
layering around the main core. The design
of the building represents multiple levels of
protection that can instill safety. In plan there
are varying grooves that are unexpected
in such a rigid form, depicting a range of
movement. It was reinforced by a ditch, a
moat, and curtain walls surrounding the main
structure.

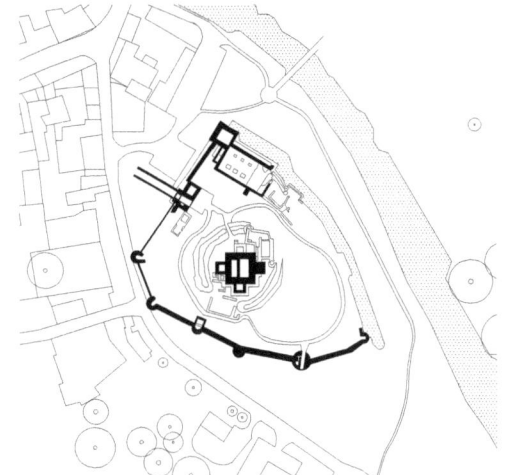
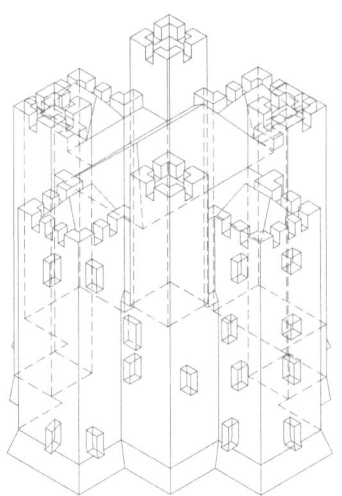

Trim Castle, Meath, Ireland 55

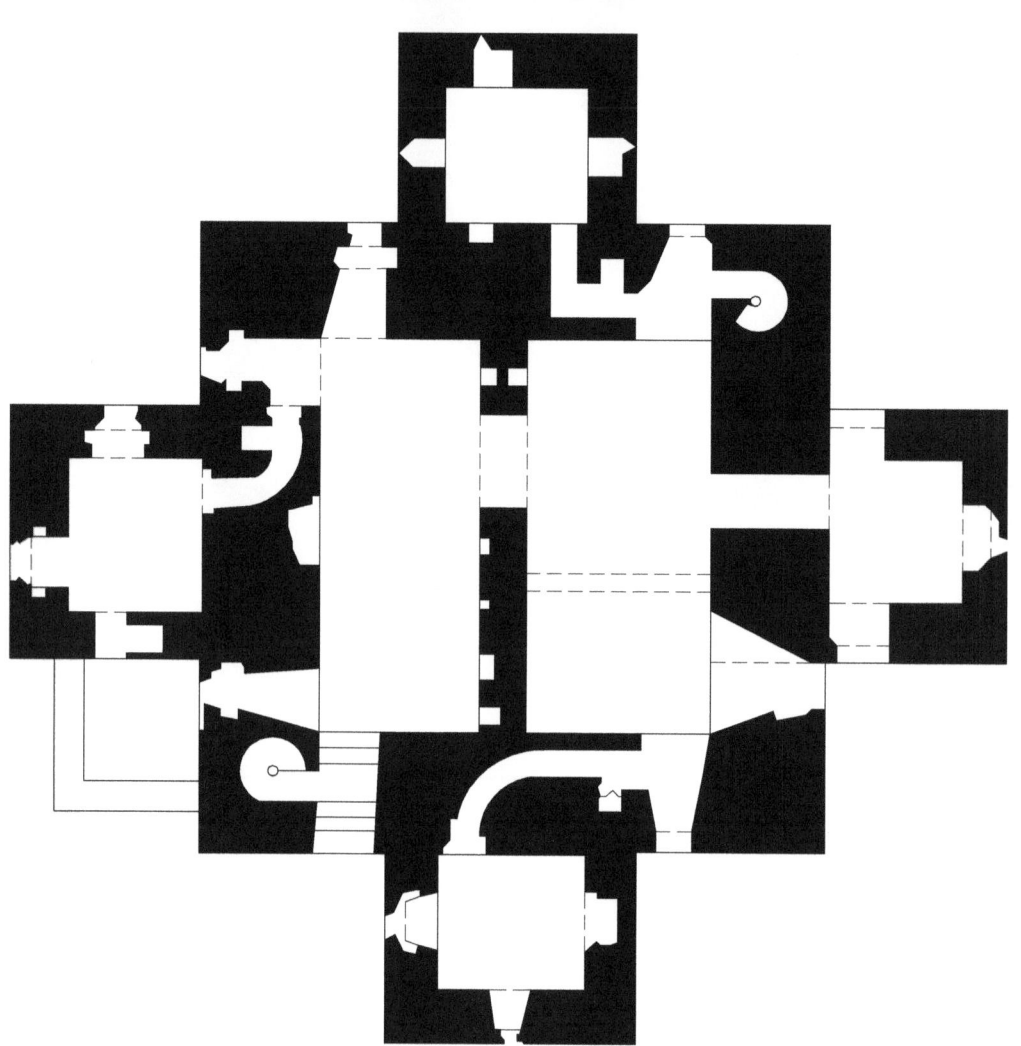

Architectural Precedents | Historic Case Studies

Trim Castle, Meath, Ireland

Trim Castle, Meath, Ireland

Tattershall Castle
Lincolnshire, England

Tattershall Castle, located in Tattershall, Lincolnshire, was designed in the 15th century by Robert Tattershall. Constructed with a crenulated stone pattern, it was eventually renovated and extended with a dense layering of brick by Lord Cromwell to flaunt his wealth and power. The 14 foot thick walls and four towers serve as tribute to this material that was not typically used for this type of construction. The castle stood at 130 feet, containing six stories, surrounded by a dual layered moat system.

At first glance this castle portrays a profound level of symmetry and dense ornamentation. With varying programmatic elements on each floor, inhabitants have a sense of security that comes from truly being hidden from the outside world. Stemming from the central core is a deep understanding of isolation. Ascending through the circulation on the corner tower allows for appreciation of the juxtaposition of density and void that comes from varying wall thicknesses. Portrayed is a curtain wall that only appears to protect.

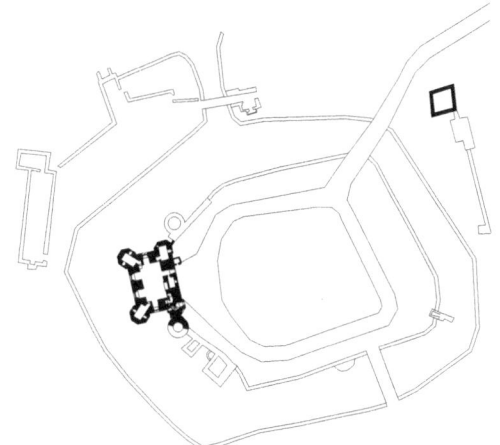

Tattershall Castle, Lincolnshire, England

61

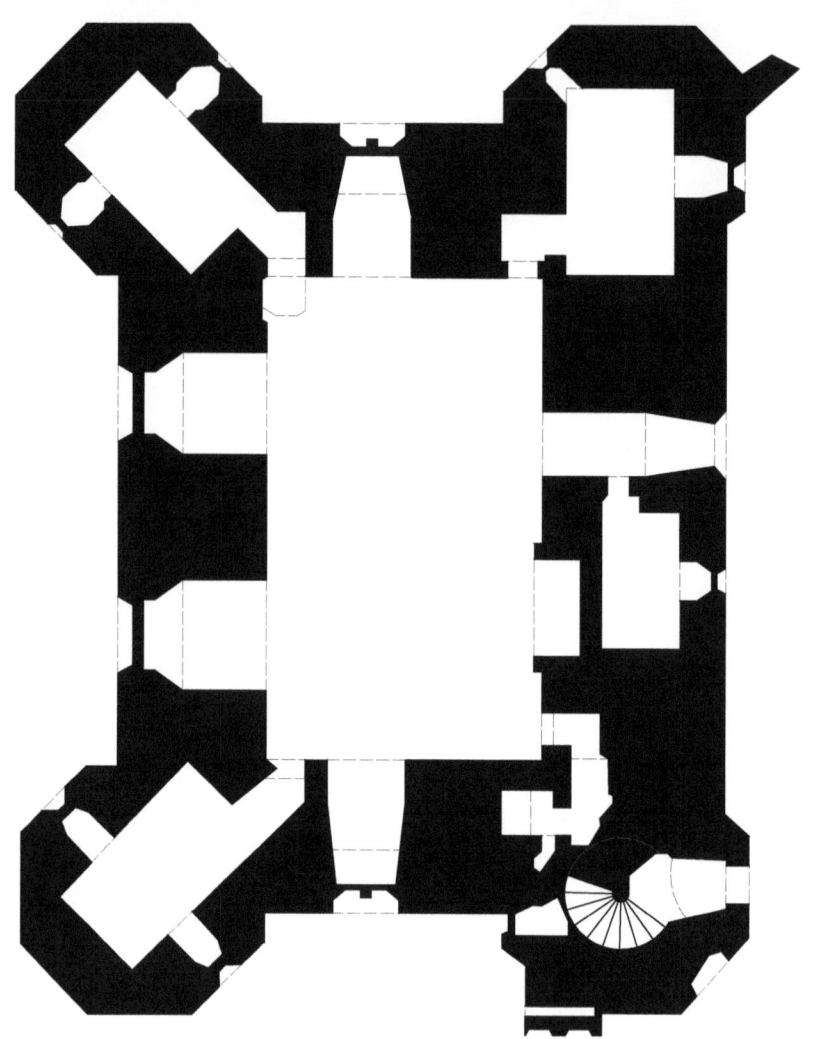

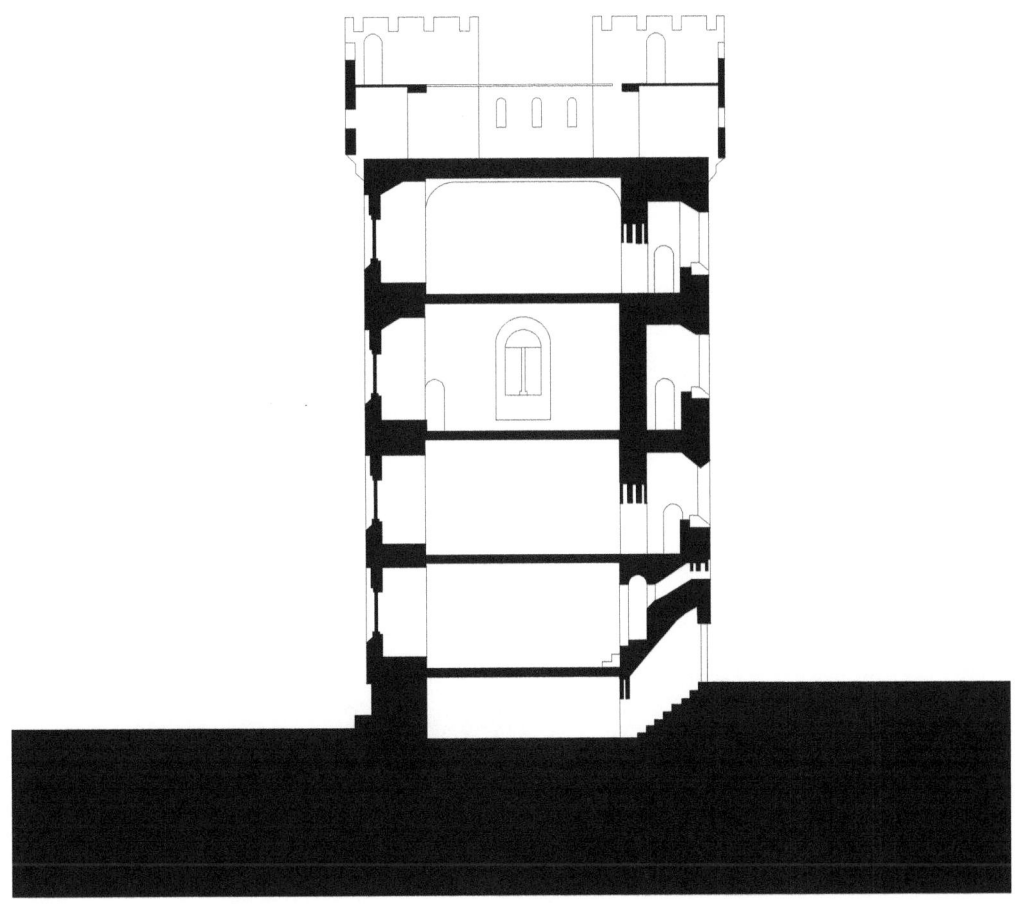

Tattershall Castle, Lincolnshire, England

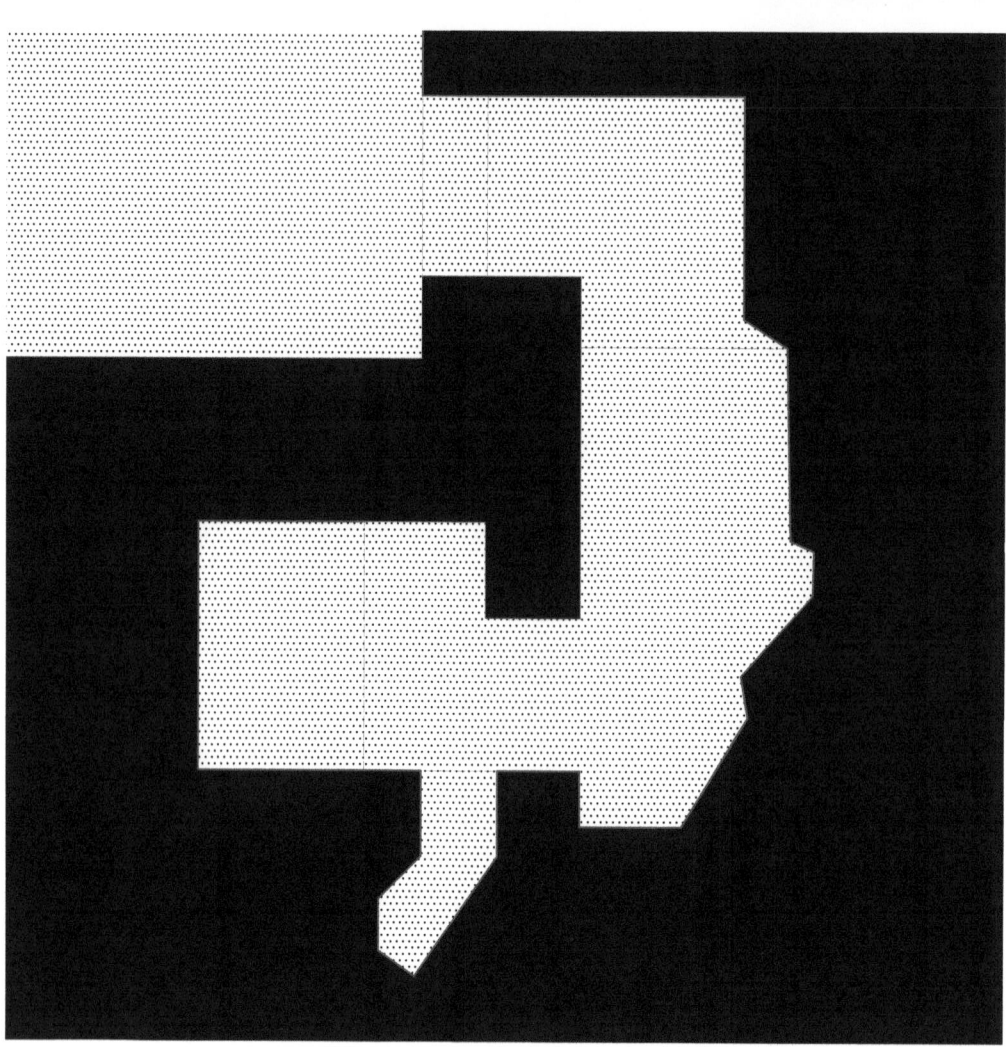

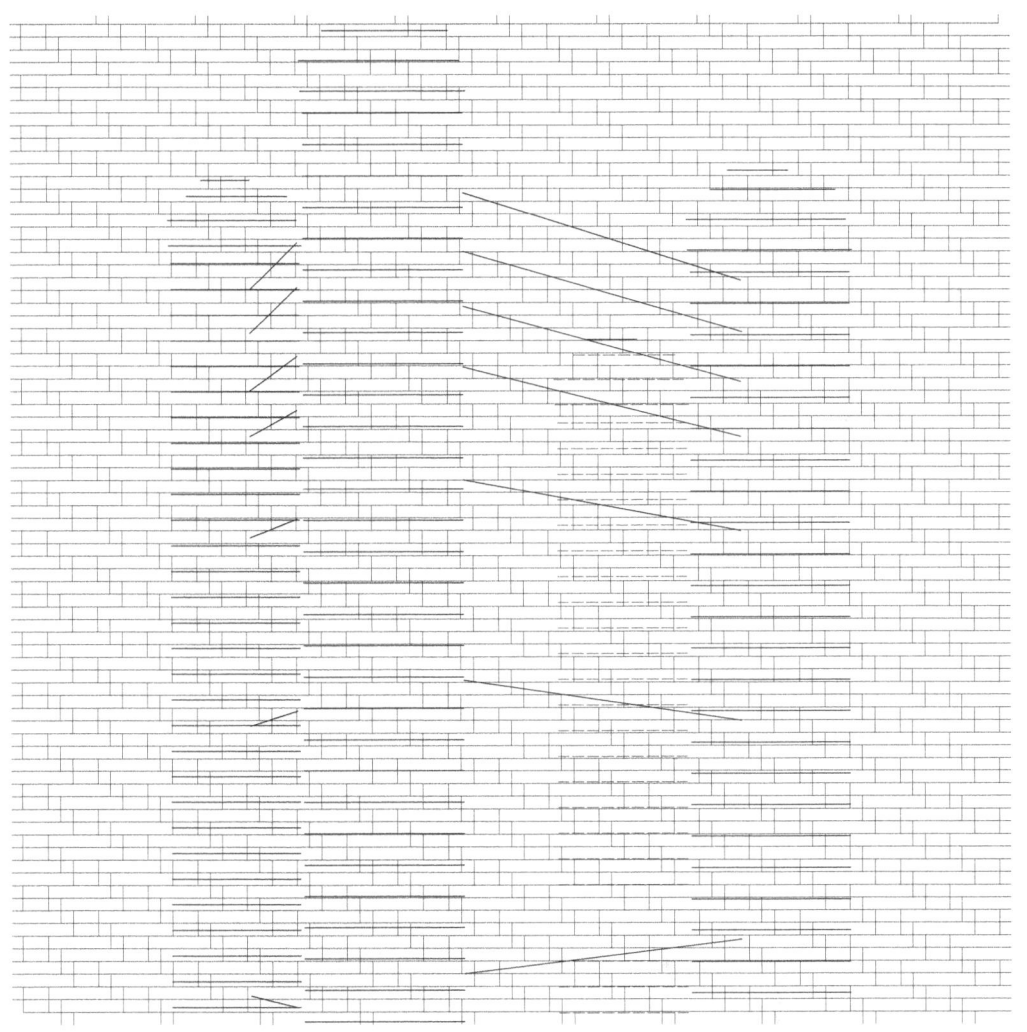

Tattershall Castle, Lincolnshire, England   65

Crichton Castle
Midlothian, Scotland

Crichton Castle, located near the village of Chrichton in Midlothian, Scotland, is known for its Italian stonework. Tucked into the mounds above the River Tyne, initially constructed in the 14th. The tower stood at about 60 feet tall, and was covered in an intricately carved diamond stone surface. Expanding as different feudal lords and their families would inhabit the land. Today the structure is comprised of four separate contiguous buildings that surround themselves around the central courtyard.

An intricate interweaving of natural light and seclusion resonates throughout the floor plan. The multiple volumes that surround the central courtyard further emphasize the layered quality of the space. A structure that was originally placed completely isolated from the rest of the world is brought together by several openings that connect the programmatic elements of the building. What would normally be considered a standalone castle acts in a way that would glorify the interior open space. Nestled in the mounds of Midlothian is this preserved juxtaposition of density and a fragility. The rich pattern of strongly geometric textured walls provides a haptic quality, hard to find in similar structures.

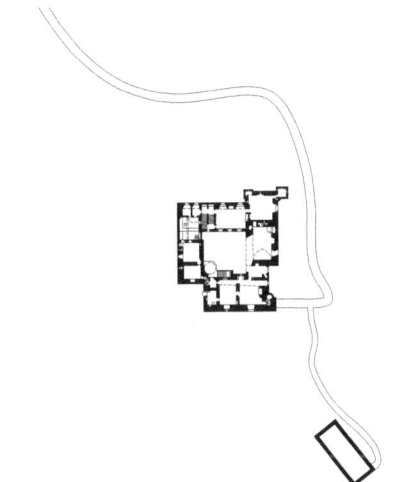
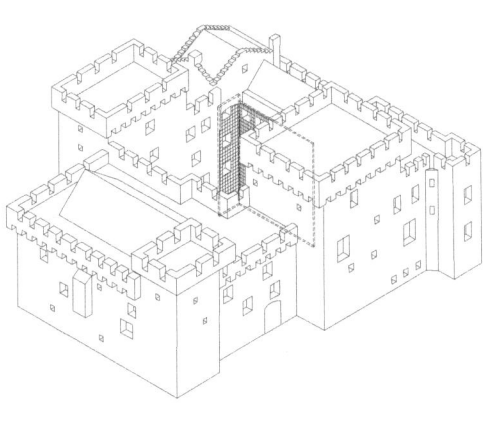

Crichton Castle, Midlothian, Scotland

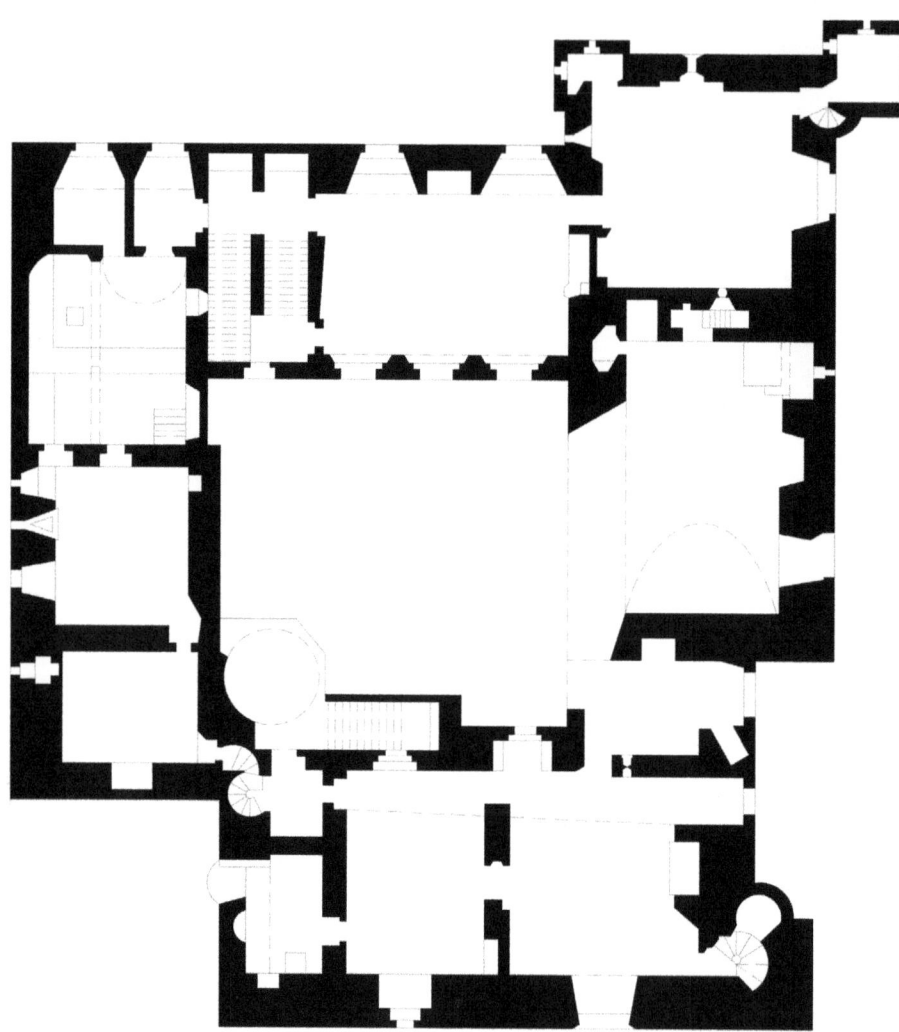

Crichton Castle, Midlothian, Scotland   69

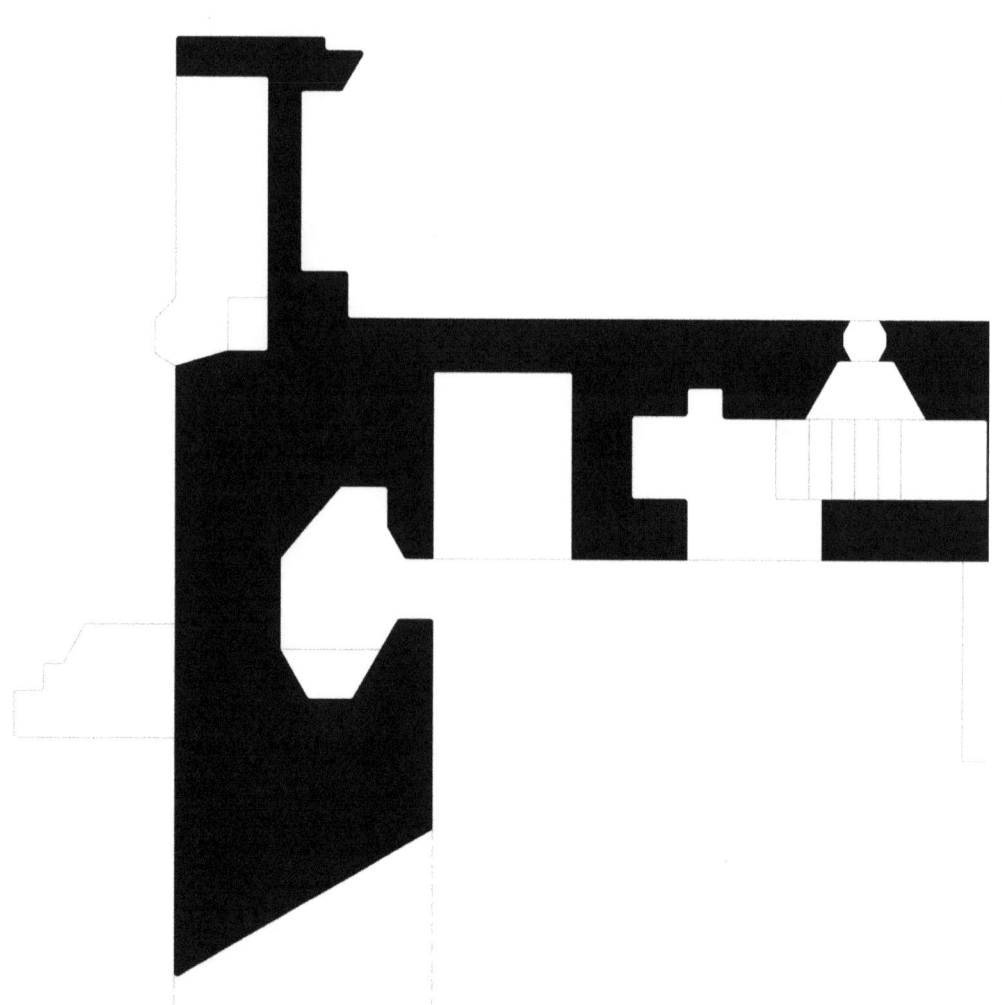

**Borthwick Castle
Gorebridge, Scotland**

Borthwick Castle, located southeast of
Edinburgh and east of Borthwick, was built
in the 15th century by Sir William Borthwick.
Constructed with Ashlar Stone, quarried from
a local source in the town of Middleton. With
battlements that reach up to 90 feet tall, this
roughly square plan was designed as a token
of gratitude towards James I. Scars from
Oliver Cromwell's artillery fire in the 1650's is
still seen to this day; the castle succumbed to
the attack after only a few cannons.

Bolstered by the embracing landscape,
the tower rises up in a seeming duplicity.
Emerging from the exterior of the castle are
glimpses of natural light that permeate the
solid voids, a subtle interplay of defense and
illumination. Rooted in a mostly square plan,
the castle's programmatic elements and
crenellations embody fortitude. The dense
15 feet thick walls are lost in the density of
the massing, appearing to be out of scale.
This shows the grandeur of the building, both
emphasizing security and comfort. A gap
seems to cut through the volume, only to state
its axial composition.

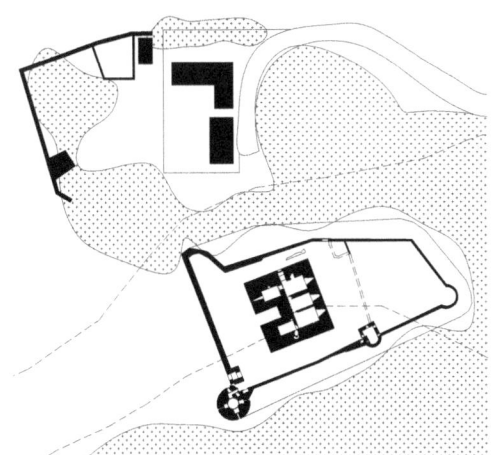
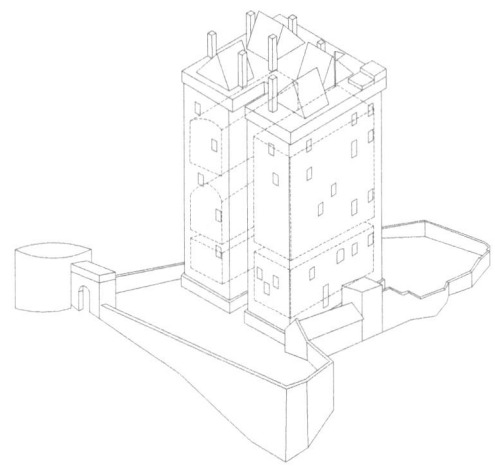

Borthwick Castle, Gorebridge, Scotland

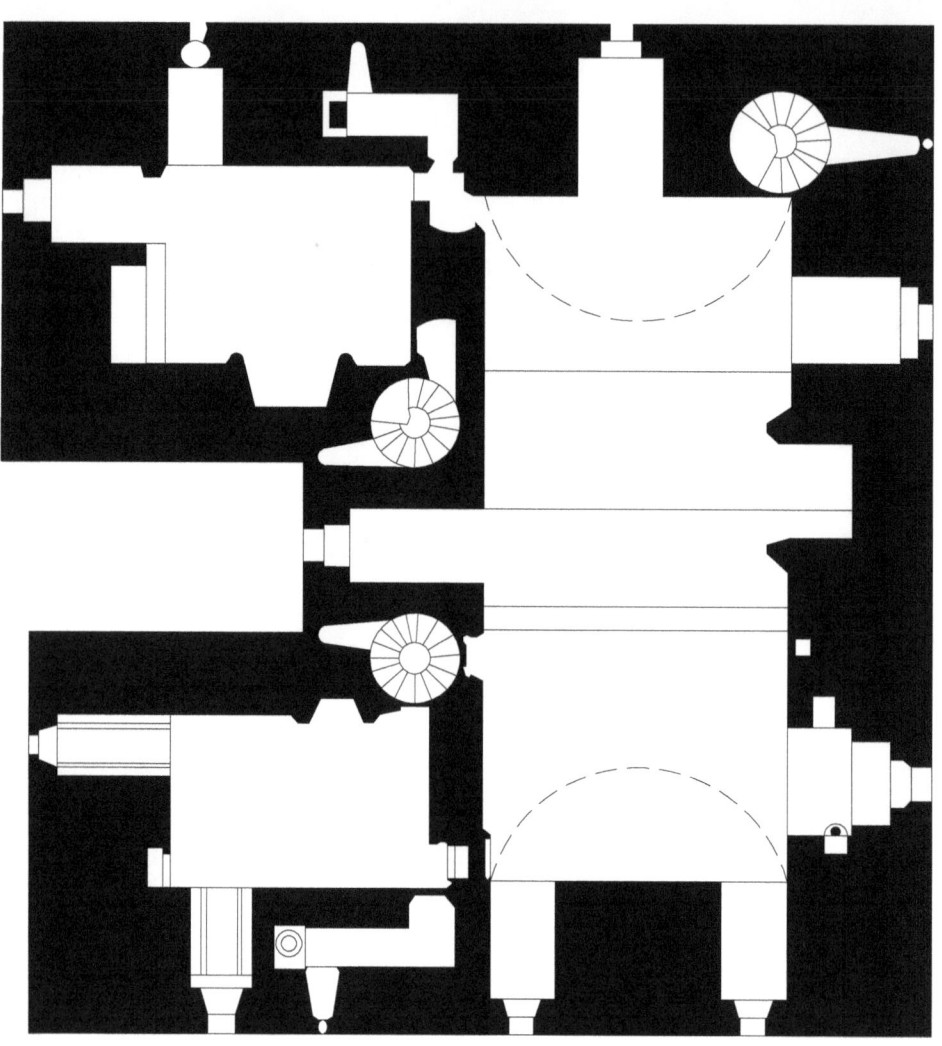

Architectural Precedents | Historic Case Studies

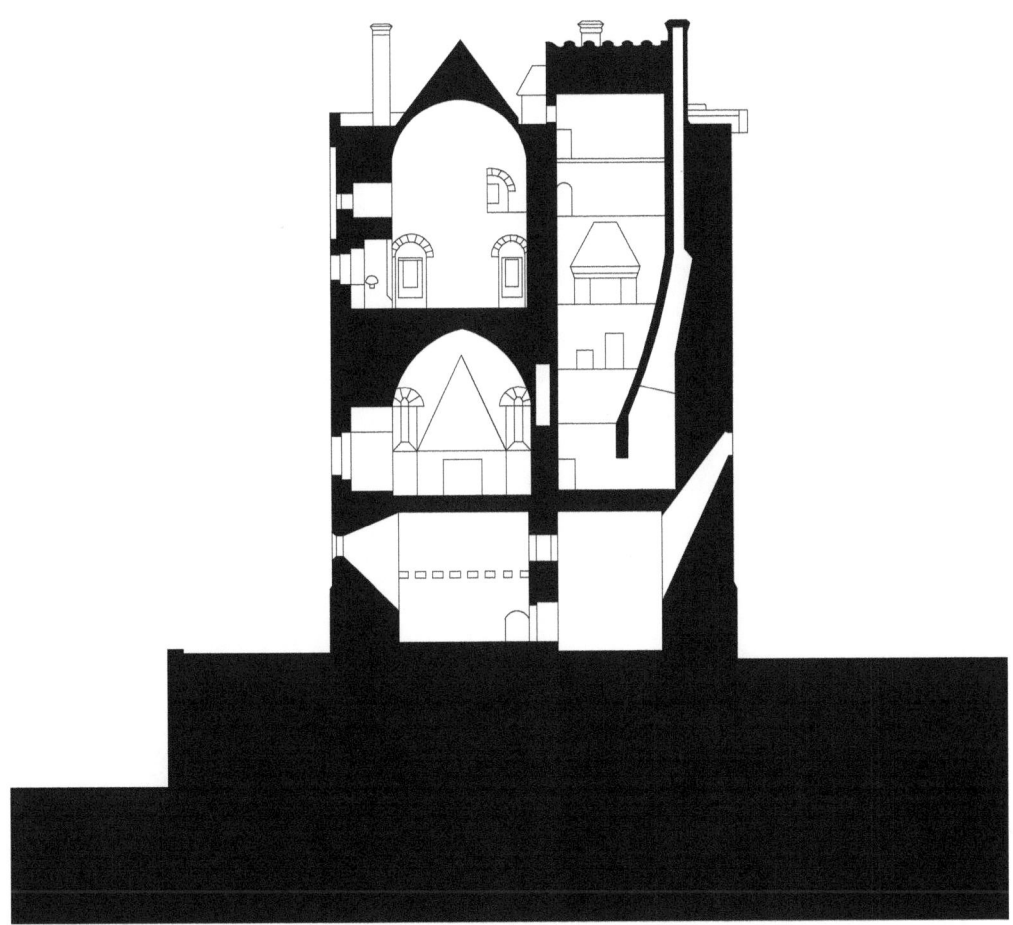

Borthwick Castle, Gorebridge, Scotland

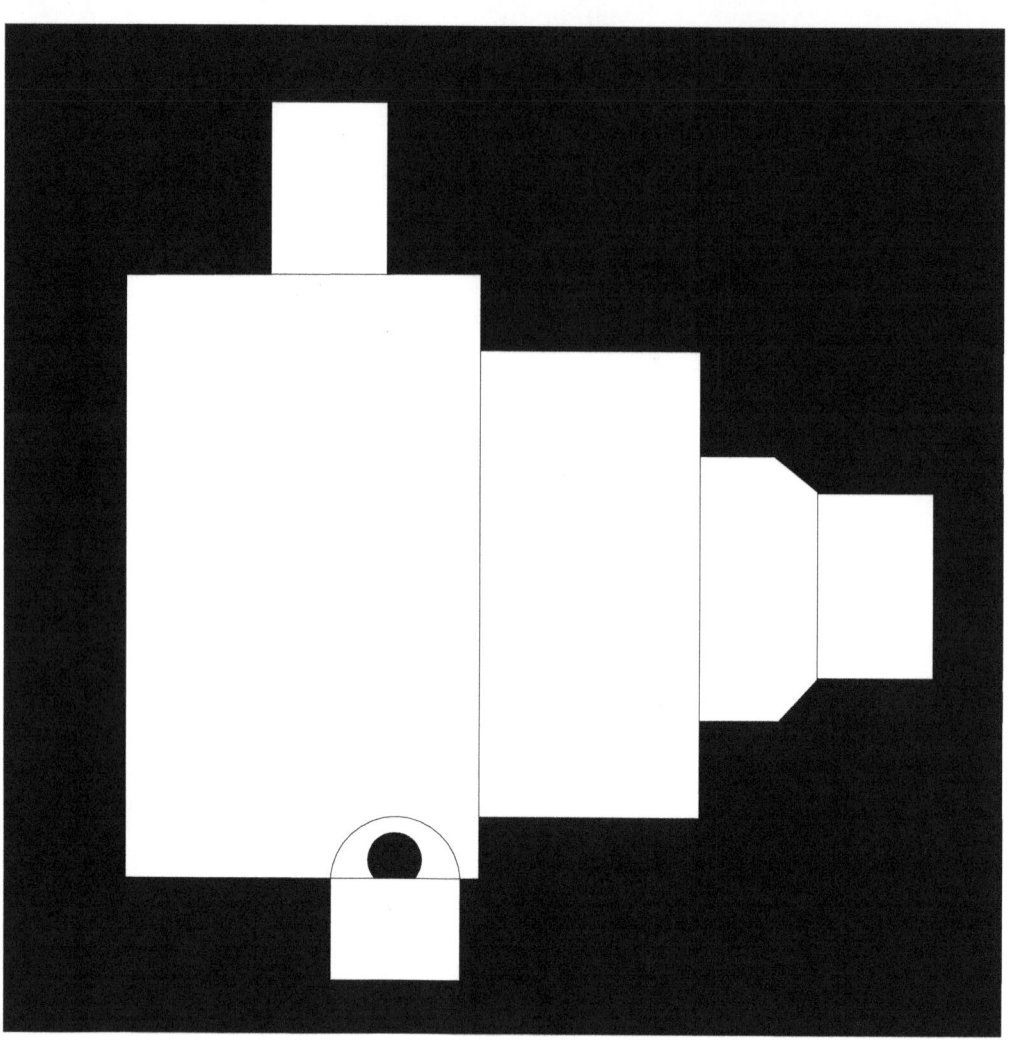

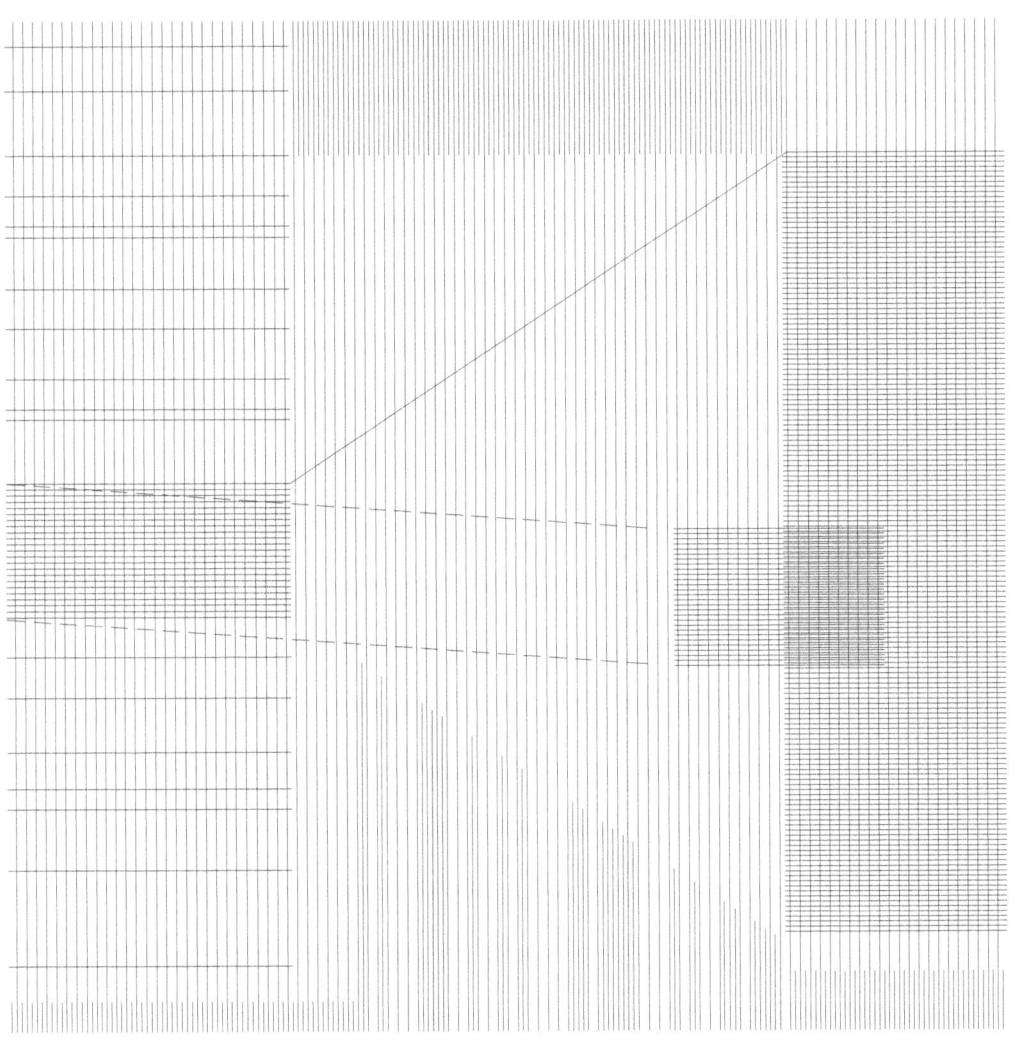

Borthwick Castle, Gorebridge, Scotland   77

Walmer Castle
Kent, England

Walmer Castle, located in Walmer, Kent, was built in the 16th century as a coastal line of defense by King Henry VIII. Designed to serve as an artillery fort, it protected against French and Roman invasions, primarily defending the Downs ship anchorage. Fortified by a central circular 75 feet in diameter keep surrounded by four bastions, each with several gun ports, all surrounded by a deep moat. It served in a three mile coastal barrier that included Deal and Sandown Castles.

Emanating from the central core is a symmetrical programmatic structure that serves as a layered fortification. A dense stone artillery castle further fortified by the coastal line that the castle was made to protect. The prominence of the interior central tower stands out above the rest in a stepped hierarchy. The section consists of an open interior space that joins all of the towers. This is a beautiful example of a mostly self-referenced construction where geometry is pushed to its limits.

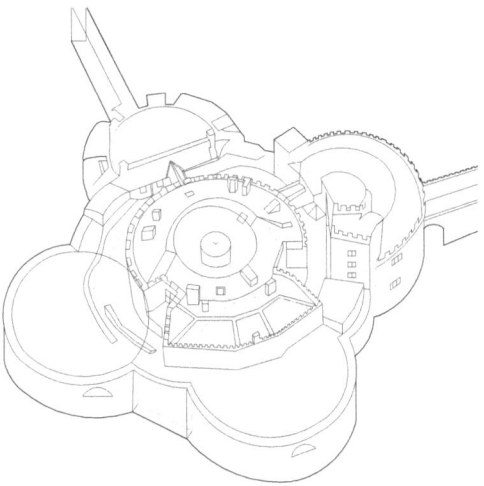

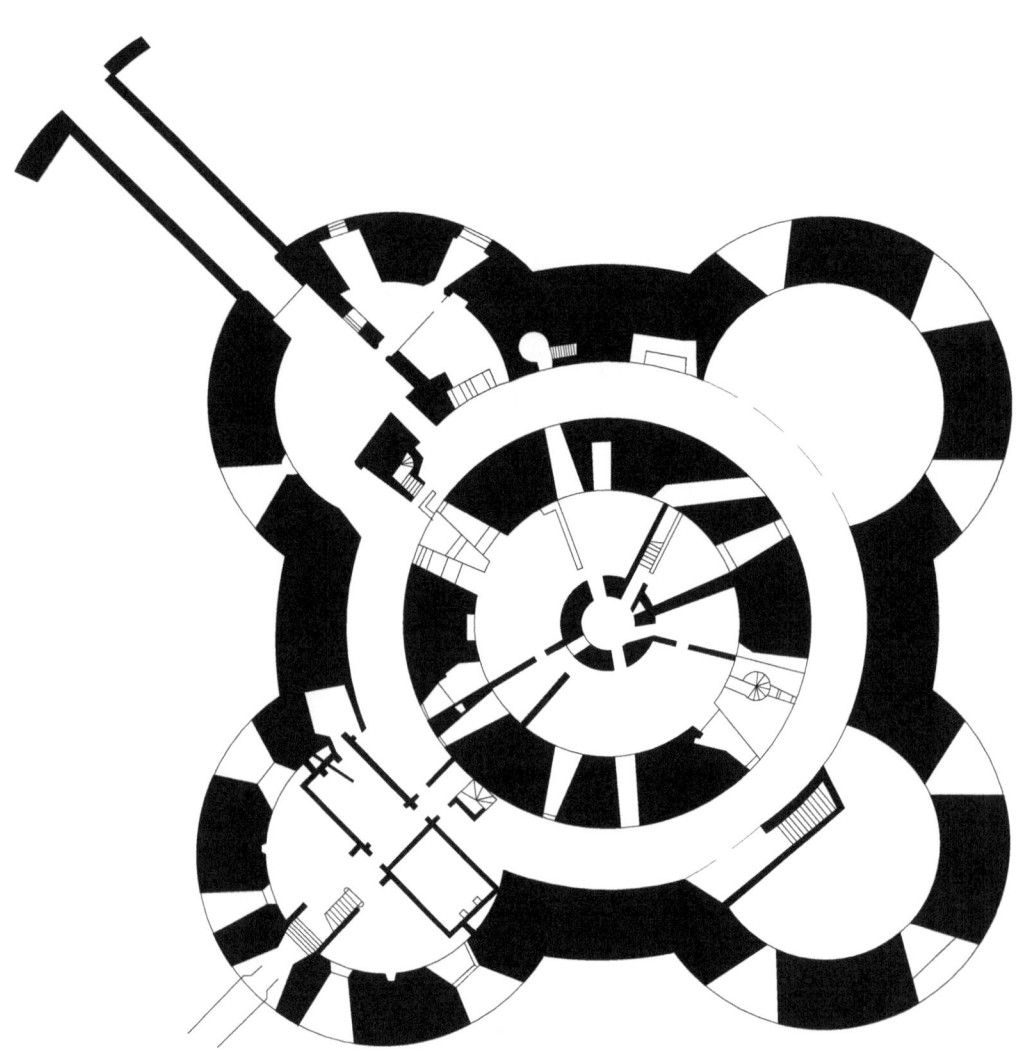

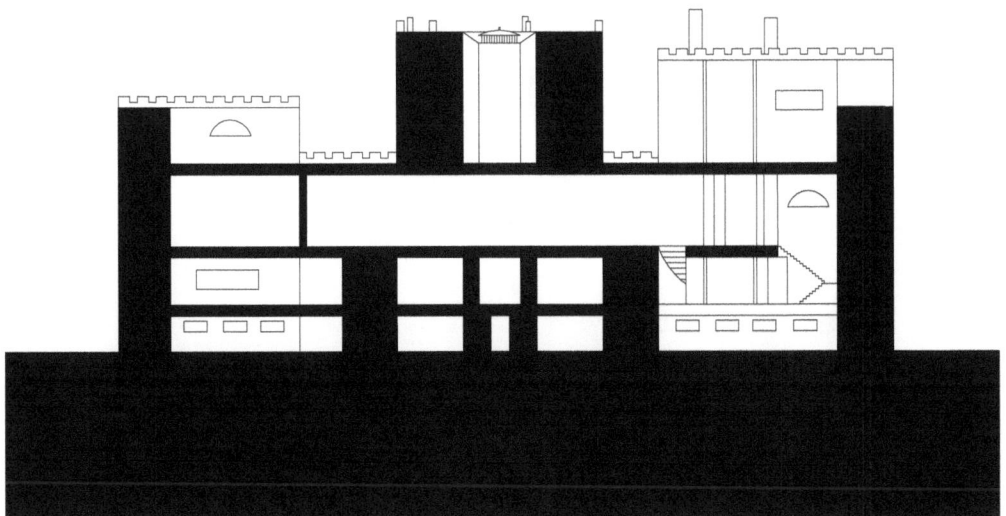

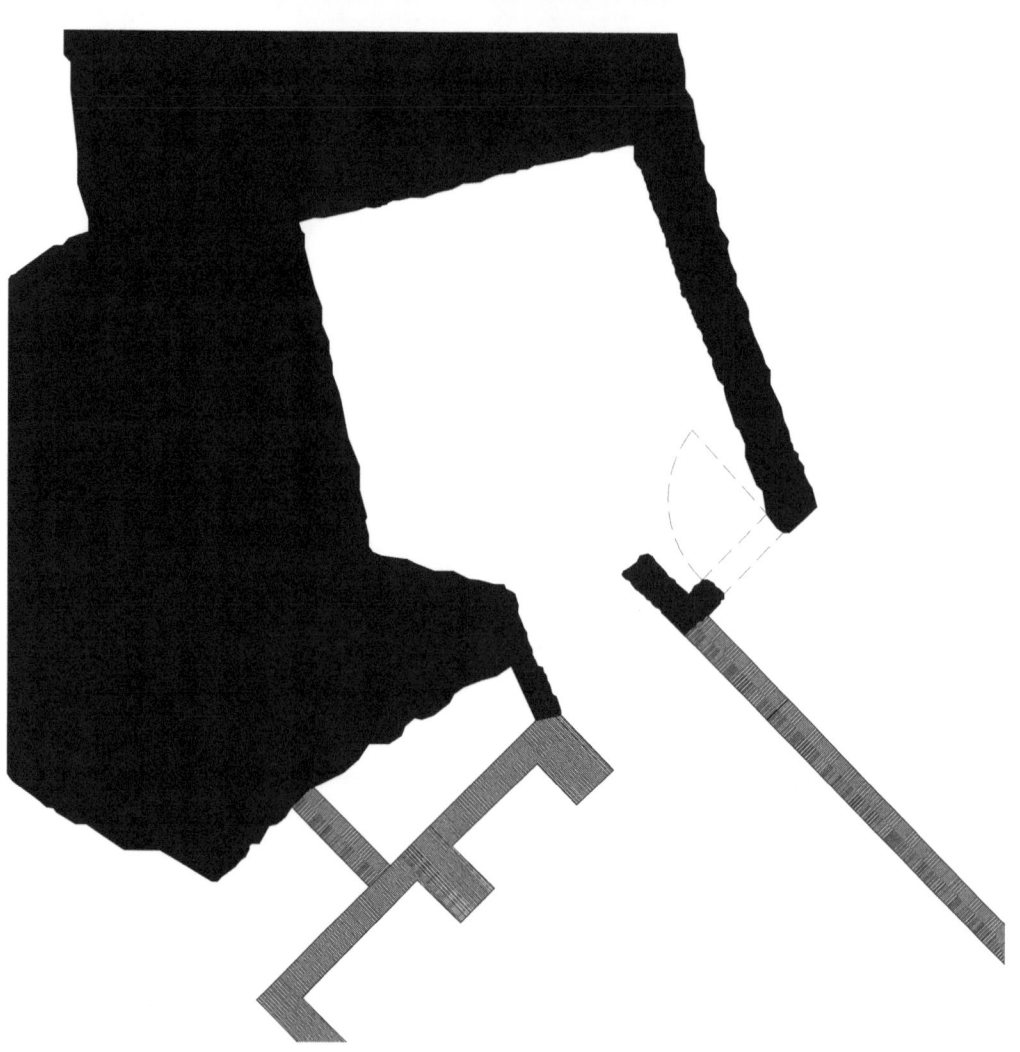

Architectural Precedents | Historic Case Studies

Walmer Castle, Kent, England

83

Deal Castle
Kent, England

The Orford Castle is located in the English county of Suffolk, and was built in the 12th century by King Henry II of England. Designed to withstand the dominating power of East Anglian Barons, as a way to guard the royal family. The castle was able to bring together the royal power of the region in support. Originally standing at a grand 90 feet, this keep and bailey castle was constructed surrounded by curtain walls and varying mounds. It eventually became the residence for several feudal lords.

The mostly preserved keep is a testament to this monolithic stone structure's defensive capabilities. Emanating from the rounded central core is a triangular configuration of towers that brings together a tight amalgamation of density in the massing. Minute moments of natural light are perforating the castle to bring life into the otherwise solid voids on the outer shell. The three towers serve as a guise that hides the open circular atrium, allowing it to safely connect with the world.

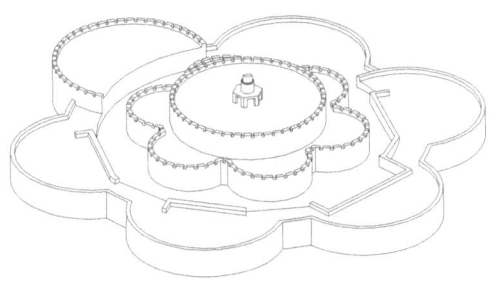

Deal Castle, Kent, England

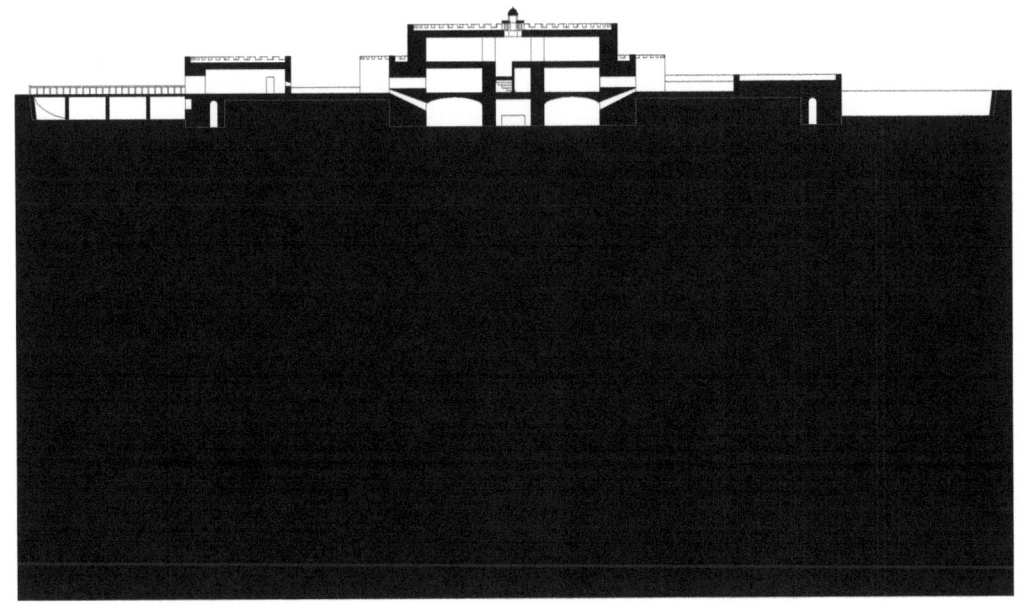

Deal Castle, Kent, England

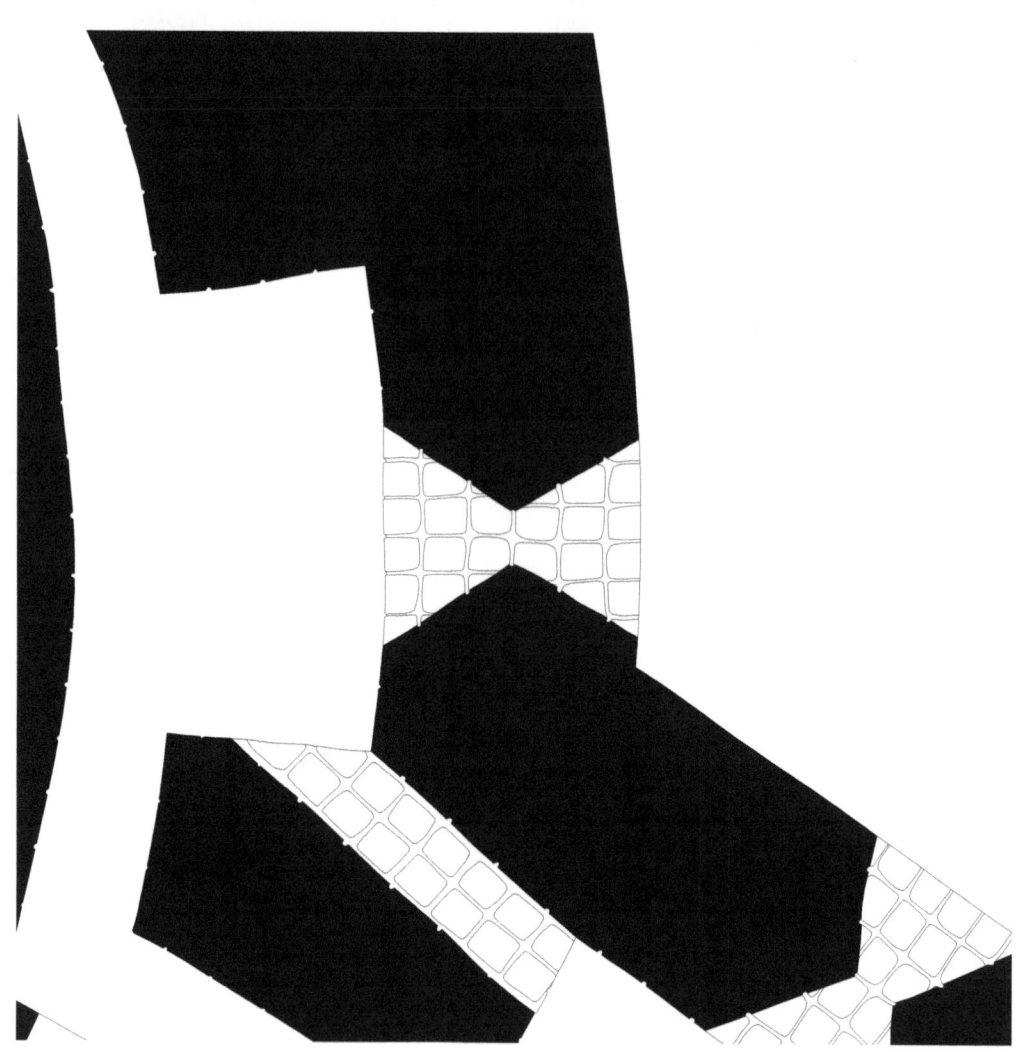

Architectural Precedents | Historic Case Studies

Deal Castle, Kent, England

Architectural Precedents
Historic Case Studies on Spatial Density and Seclusion

Spanish Castles

41.596937, -4.114416

Peñafiel Castle
Valladolid, Spain

Peñafiel Castle rises atop a narrow limestone ridge in Valladolid, extending a length of 210 meters while maintaining a width of 35 meters, producing an oblong form that can be compared to the keel of a ship. Originally established in the 10th century, its current configuration reflects major 15th century reconstructions under Don Pedro Girón. The Gothic military style castle is built primarily from Campaspero stone. Anchored at the midpoint of the ridge is a 34 meter high Torre del Homenaje.

The elongated mass of Peñafiel reads as both wall and vessel. Its tight proportions stretch across the terrain, responding directly to the topographic constraints of the ridge. The mass is reductive yet forceful, with minimal apertures and thick continuous masonry evoking a defensive skin. Its single formal gesture splits the plan to be nearly symmetrical. Circulation along the upper walls maintains the sense of perimeter control, while interior voids remain isolated within the larger mass. Ornament is sparse and embedded, seen in the rhythm of turrets and the articulation of battlements. Performing through alignment and compression, the castle's strength is found in restraint over articulation.

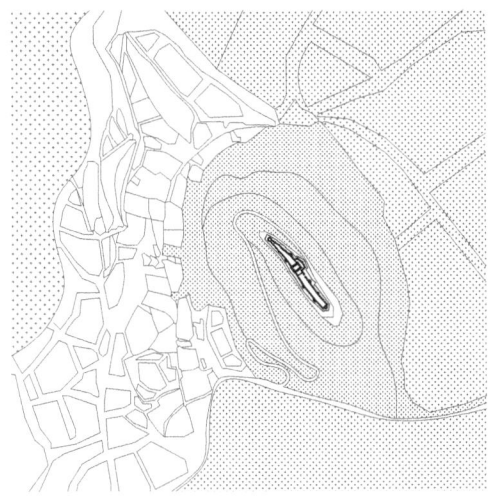
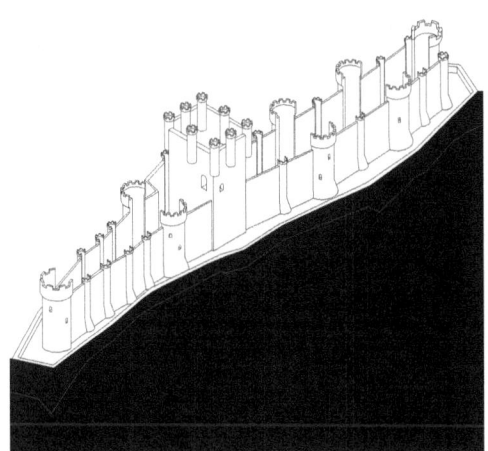

Peñafiel Castle, Valladolid, Spain

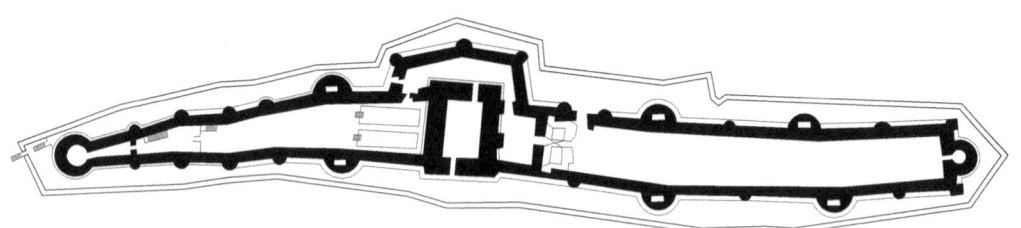

Architectural Precedents | Historic Case Studies

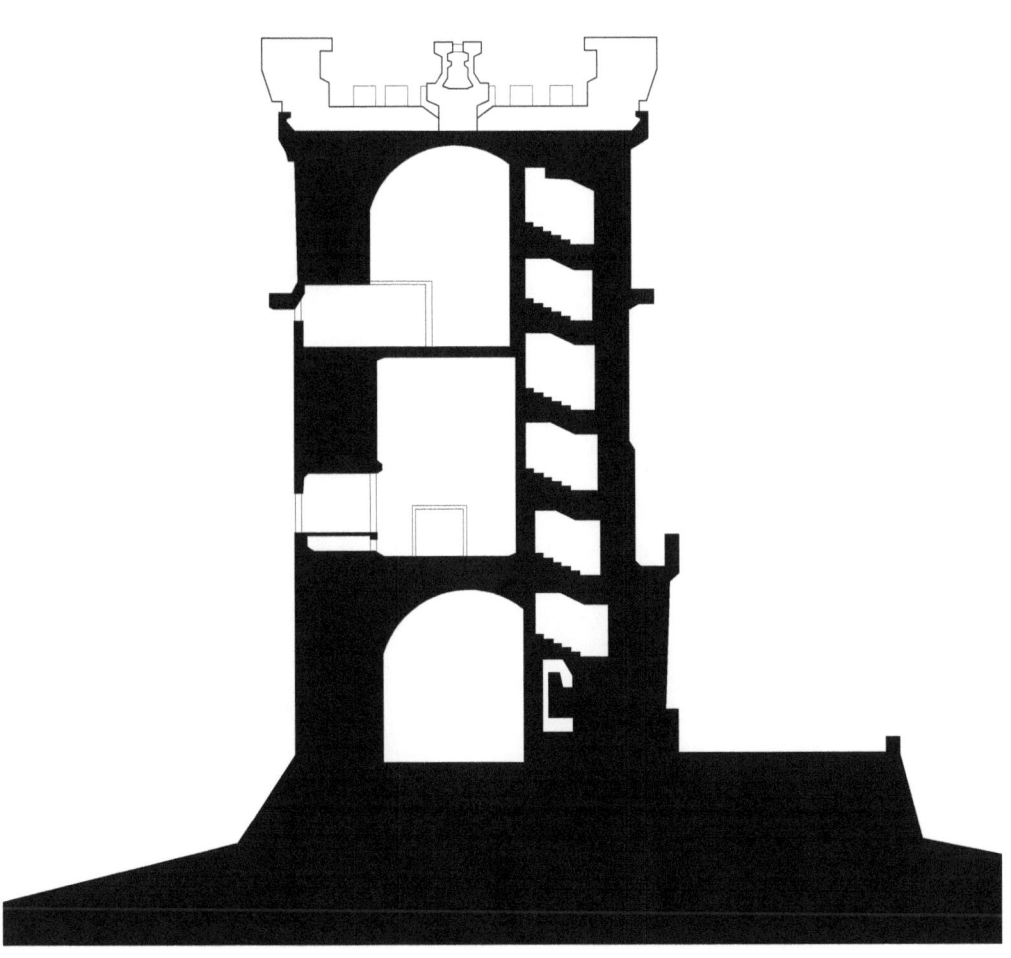

Peñafiel Castle, Valladolid, Spain   95

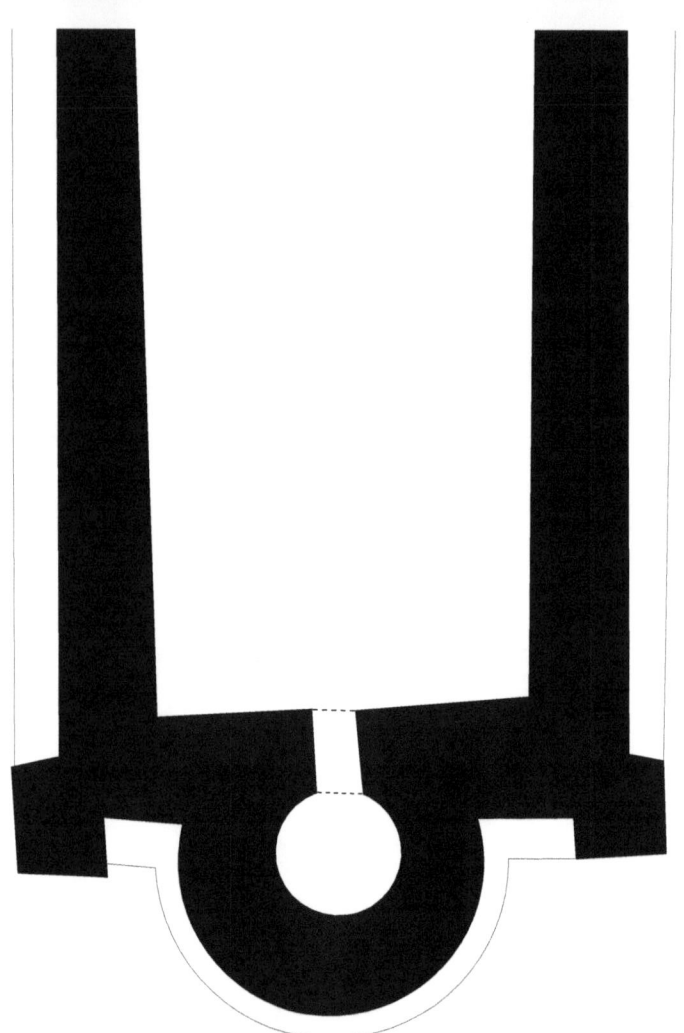

Architectural Precedents | Historic Case Studies

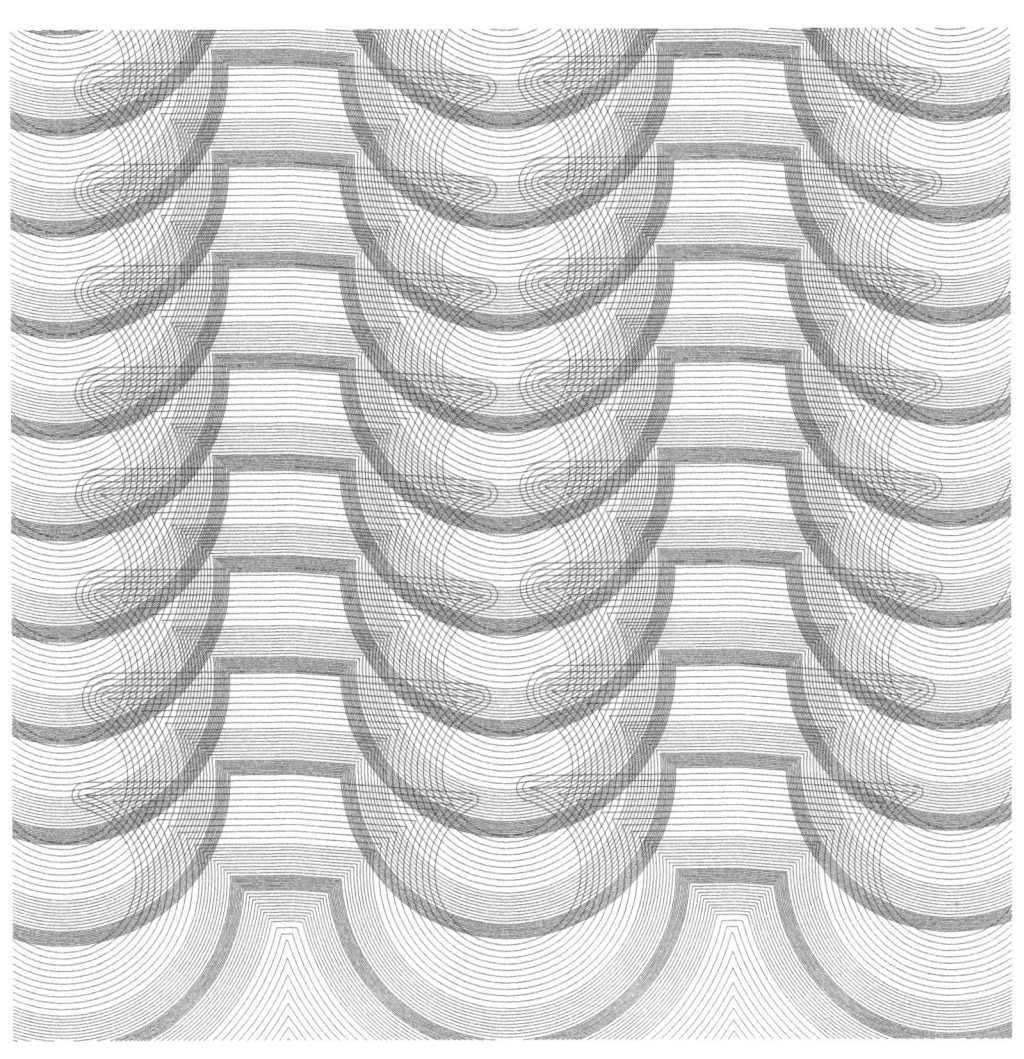

Burgalimar Castle
Jaén, Spain

Built in 967 AD under Caliph Al-Hakam II, Burgalimar Castle is one of the oldest surviving fortresses in Europe. It was strategically constructed atop Cerro del Cueto in Baños de la Encina, guarding the Guadalquivir Valley and the trade routes to Córdoba. Its oval-shaped enclosure, spanning 100 meters by 50 meters, is reinforced by fourteen original square towers, with a fifteenth, the Torre del Homenaje, added by the Castilians in 1466. It was declared a National Historic Monument in 1931.

The tapial walls, made from compacted lime, sand, and clay, have withstood centuries of conflict. Time has fused the castle with the land, its weathered tapial walls blending into the rugged terrain. Each tower, standing in defiant rhythm, forms a silent dialogue with the past, recalling both Almohad resilience and Castilian conquest. The southern gate, flanked by two towers, bears horseshoe arches and remnants of defensive chambers where stones and boiling liquids were once dropped on invaders. Inside, a cistern, divided by pillars, hints at the fortress's self-sufficiency. Sunlight moves across its battlements, casting shifting patterns that echo the passage of time.

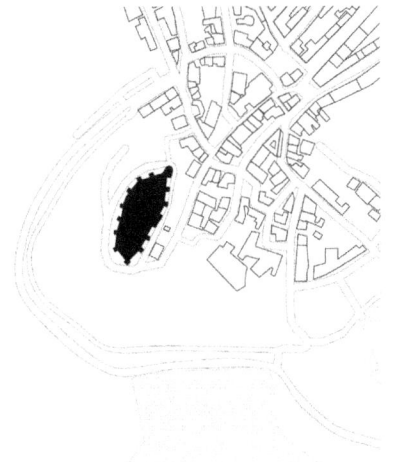
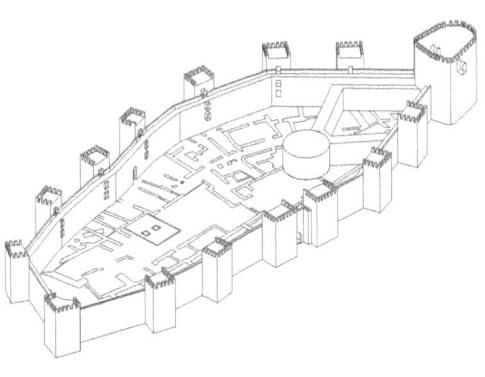

Burgalimar Castle, Jaén, Spain

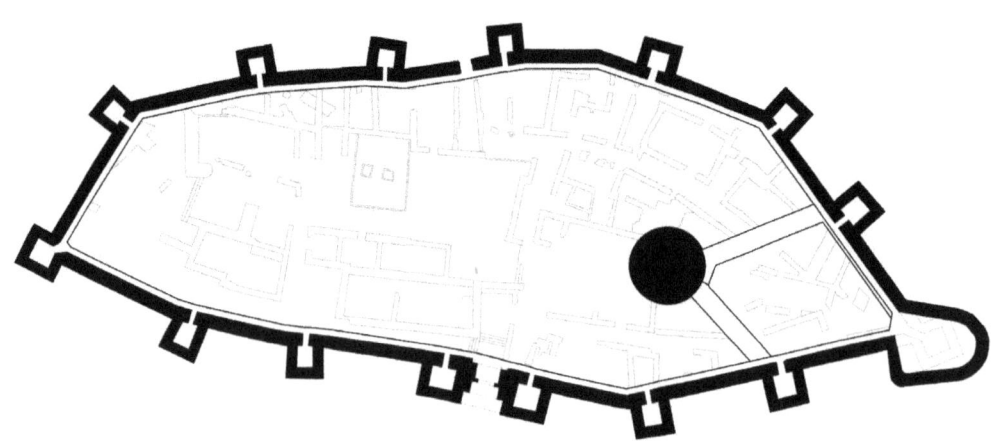

Burgalimar Castle, Jaén, Spain

Burgalimar Castle, Jaén, Spain

Javier Castle
Navarra, Spain

Constructed in the 10th century, originally only a rectilinear defensive tower made to watch over both kingdoms of Navarra and Aragon, this castle has undergone major changes. With renovations in the 12th and 13th century the most prominent changes followed the towers partial destruction in the 15th century, when the palatial birthplace of Saint Francis Javier was built. Following the final additions and restoration in the early 20th century, the castle still holds its military fortifications and original ornamentation.

This rugged, quiet castle has shown an unwavering strength that battles the test of time. Its weathered stone is carved from the earth, the staggered fortifications unfold in a layered ascension. Each wall reinforces the rhythmic pulse of defense, its sentinel towers asymmetrical and unyielding. The silhouette of the crenellations that break the view of the horizon, have been softened by the elements that have shaped these lands for centuries. Within the walls, the weight of devotion lingers, this is not just a fortress, but a place of pilgrimage, where faith and fortification intertwine. Here, history is felt with every subsequent stone, in the shadowed archways and worn battlements that whisper of a past that refuses to fade.

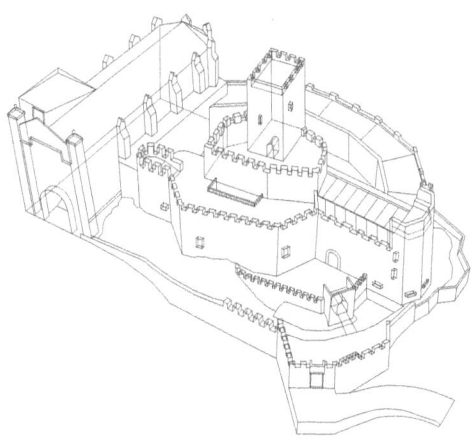

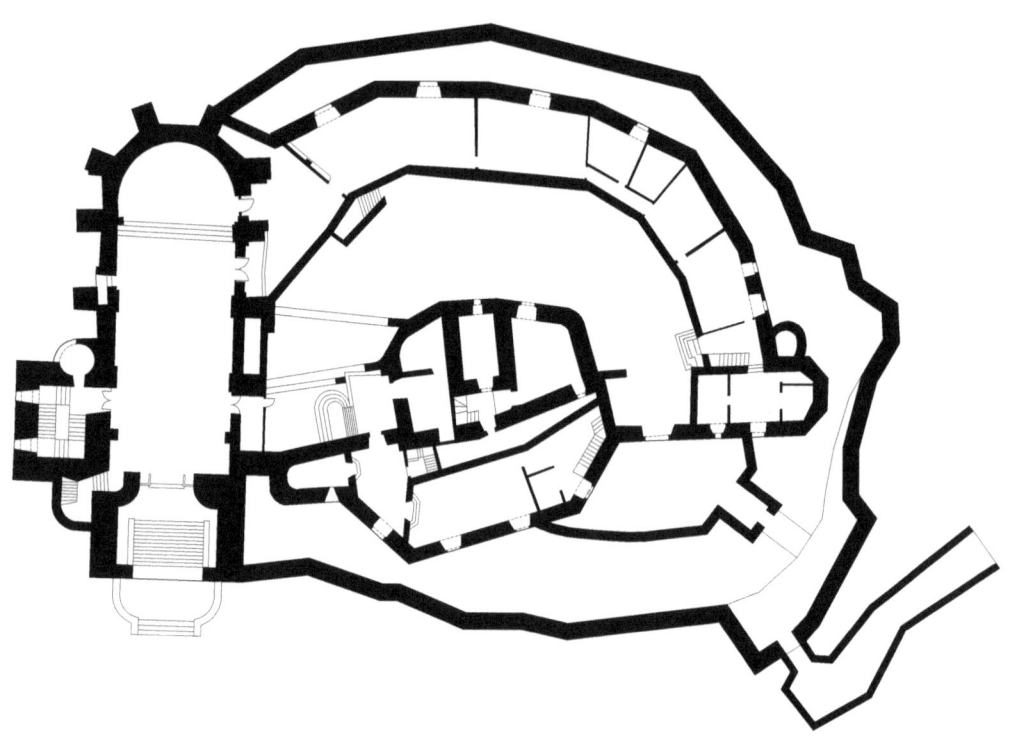

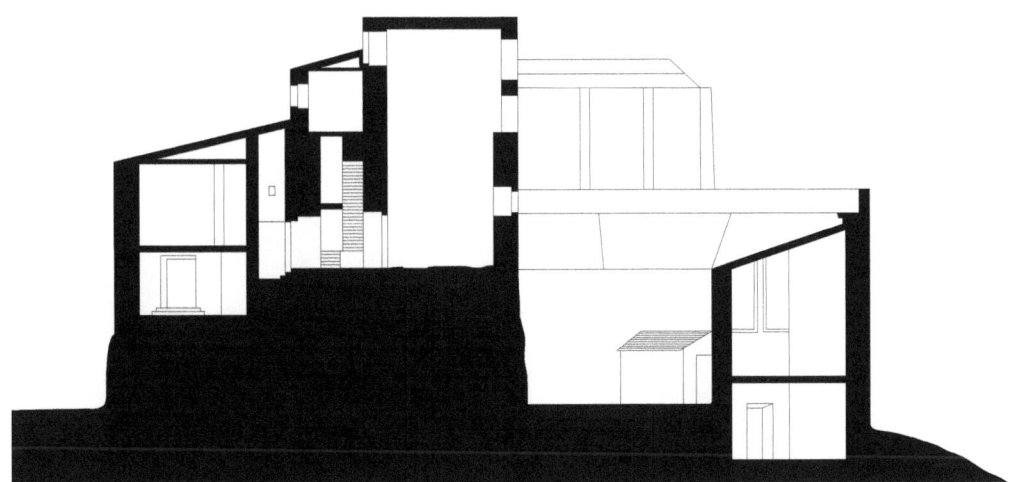

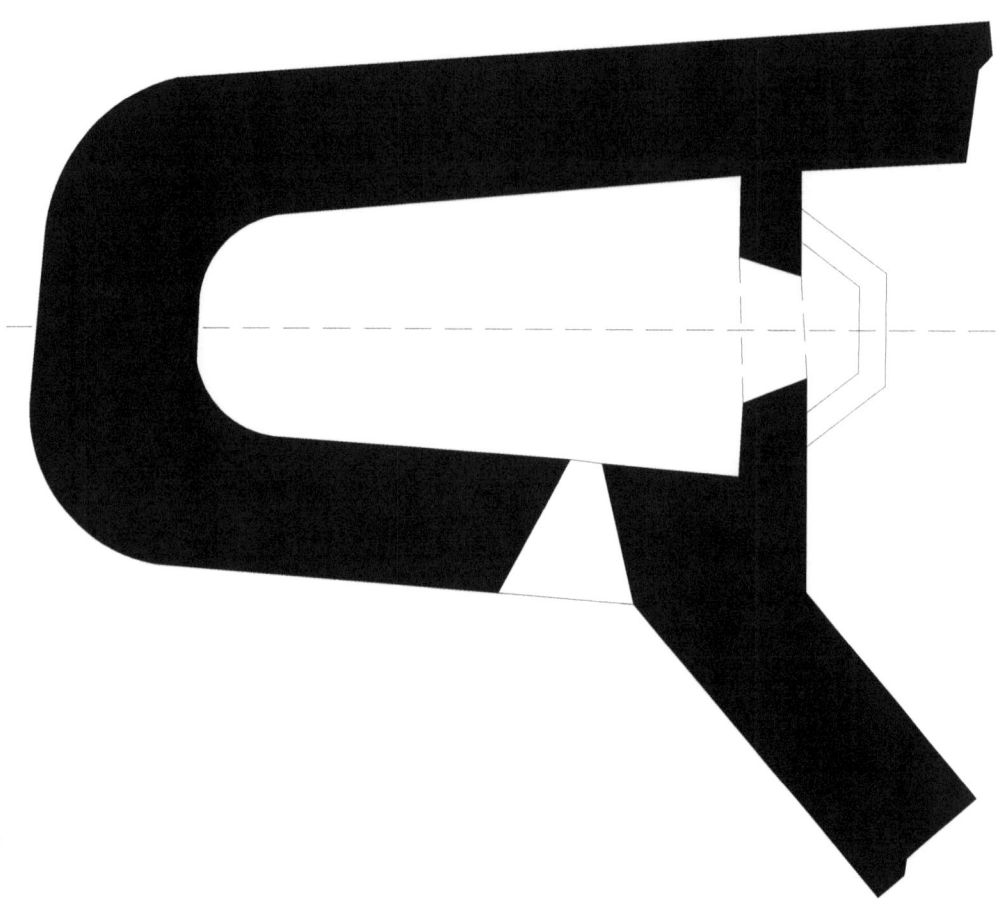

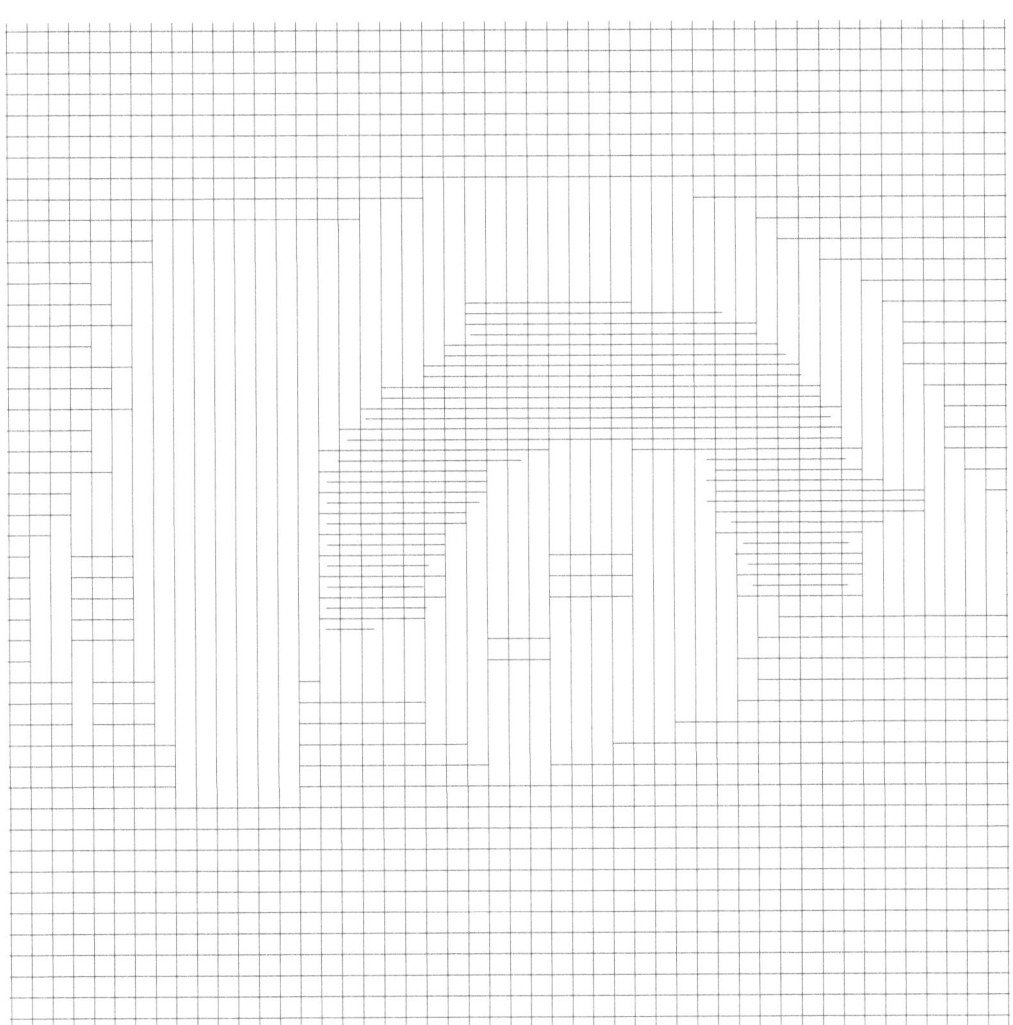

Loarre Castle
Huesca, Spain

Perched on a rocky outcrop overlooking the Hoya de Huesca, this castle was built in the early 11th century by Sando III de Navarre. A preserved Romanesque fortress with an irregular layout, enclosed by double curtain walls and fortified cylindrical towers. Within its walls lies the 12th century Church of Santa Maria. Originally a royal residence, it later became an Austinian monastery under Sanoho Ramírez. The castle played a crucial role in the Reconquista, reinforcing its military and religious significance.

Rising from the limestone ridge, Loarre's silhouette is carved by time, its towers standing like sentinels over the vast Aragonese plains. The castle does not impose itself upon the land; instead, it embraces the rock, its walls weaving through the landscape in an organic symbiosis of stone and sky. The Queen's Tower, with its twin-arched windows, whispers of lost grandeur, while the Torre del Homenaje, once connected by a wooden bridge, looms in quiet defiance. Inside, the stone surfaces worn smooth by centuries of devotion and war. Loarre is a monument to resilience, hosting the doctrine of form follows function, as apertures carved from the facade linger like silent witnesses to the lives once sheltered within.

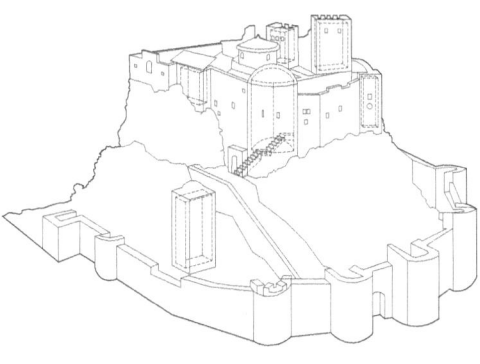

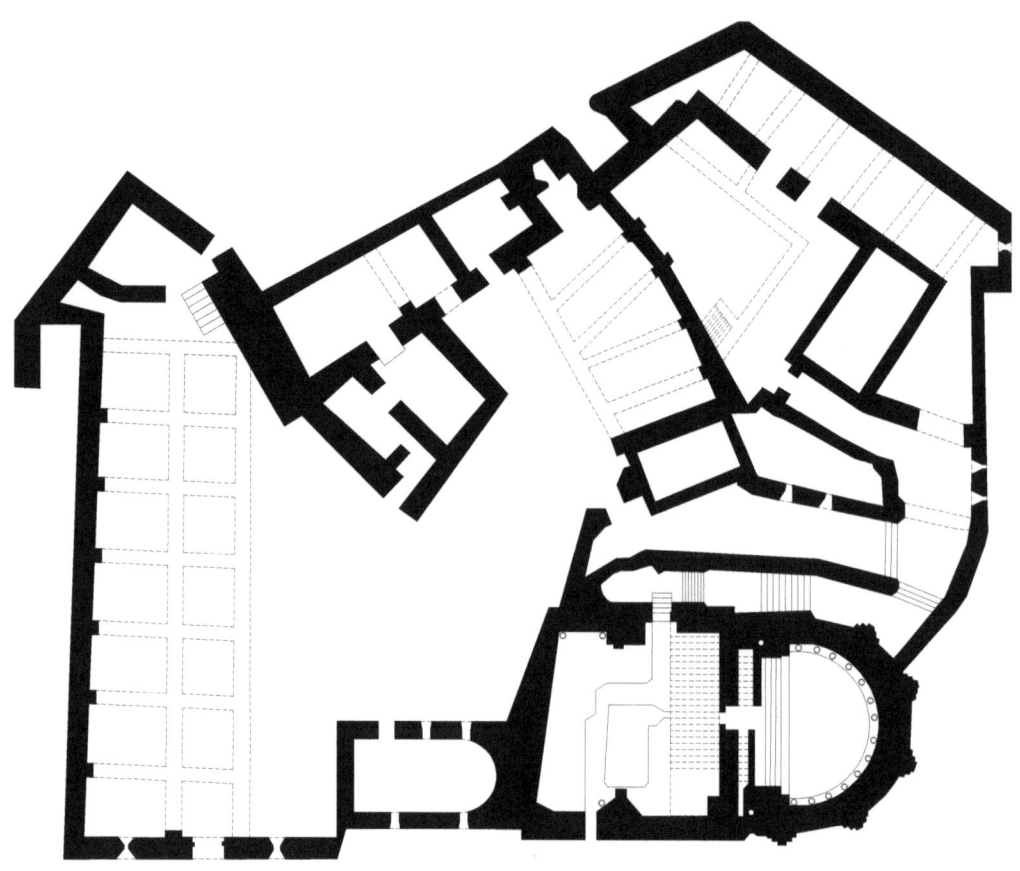

Loarre Castle, Huesca, Spain

Architectural Precedents | Historic Case Studies

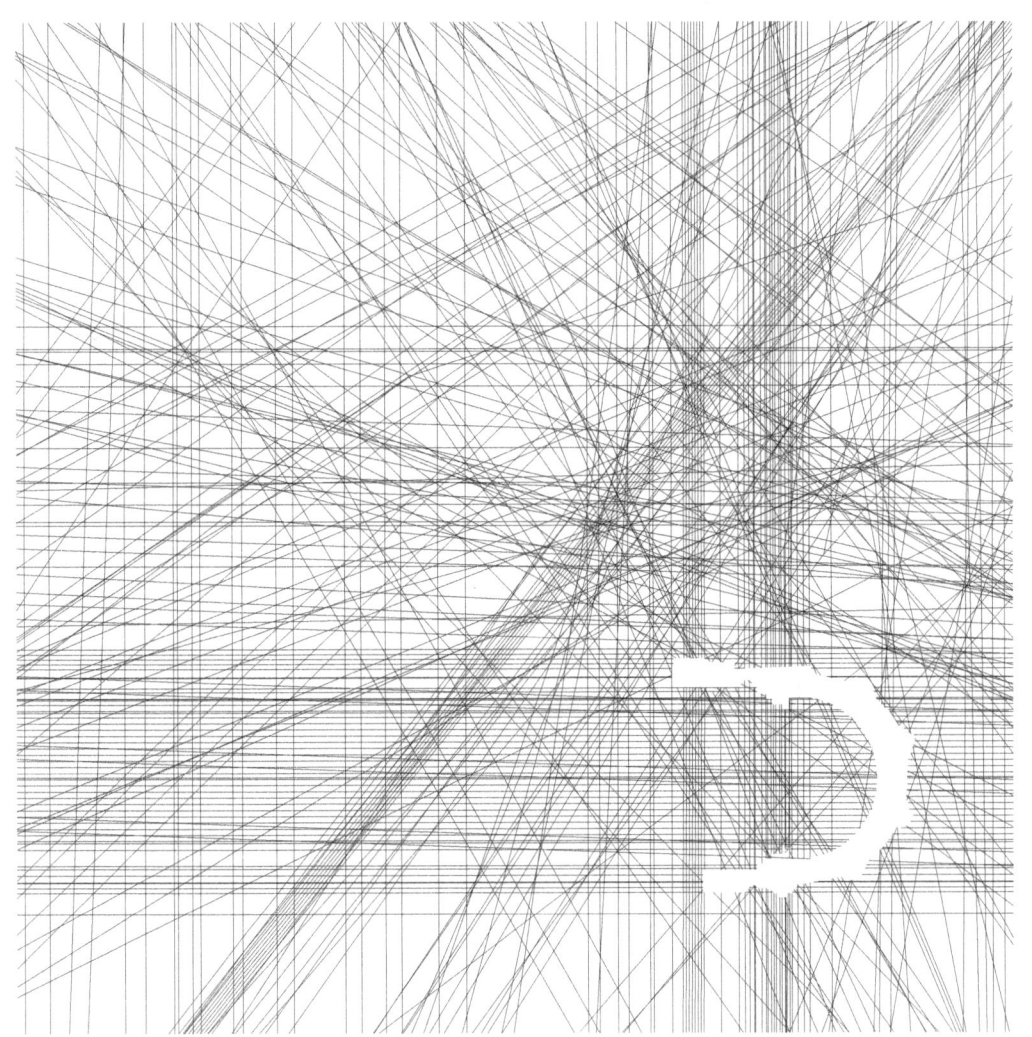

Loarre Castle, Huesca, Spain

38.631895, -0.861090

Villena Castle
Alicante, Spain

Built as a refuge for the Muslim population during the end of the 12th century, Villena Castle was established on a hill in the Town of Villena, in the province of Alicante, Spain. Remaining from this period are the first two floors and tall pronounced inner wall built from rammed earth masonry. Once the Pacheco family was under rule, fortifications were added to this fortress originally built by the Almohad Empire, adding two floors and a second outer wall containing twelve towers made of stone.

These hierarchical massings protrude from the earth, their rigid geometry accentuating a primordial need for protection. The castle's dense tectonic composition, layered in deliberate succession, stands as an unyielding bastion against intrusion. The concentric plan, an orchestration of inner and ascending walls, reinforces a rectilinear presence. An imposing cuboid structure that looms with an air of timeless defiance. The towers, rising at its corners, serve as sentinels of vigilance, their vantage points commanding the landscape beyond. Within this fortress of stone, the weight of history is palpable, its fortifications whispering the echoes of conflict and endurance.

 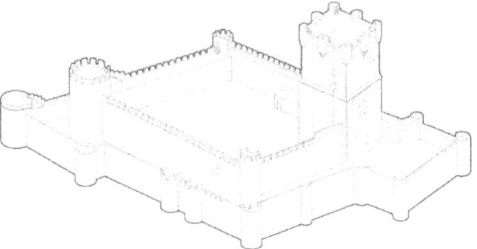

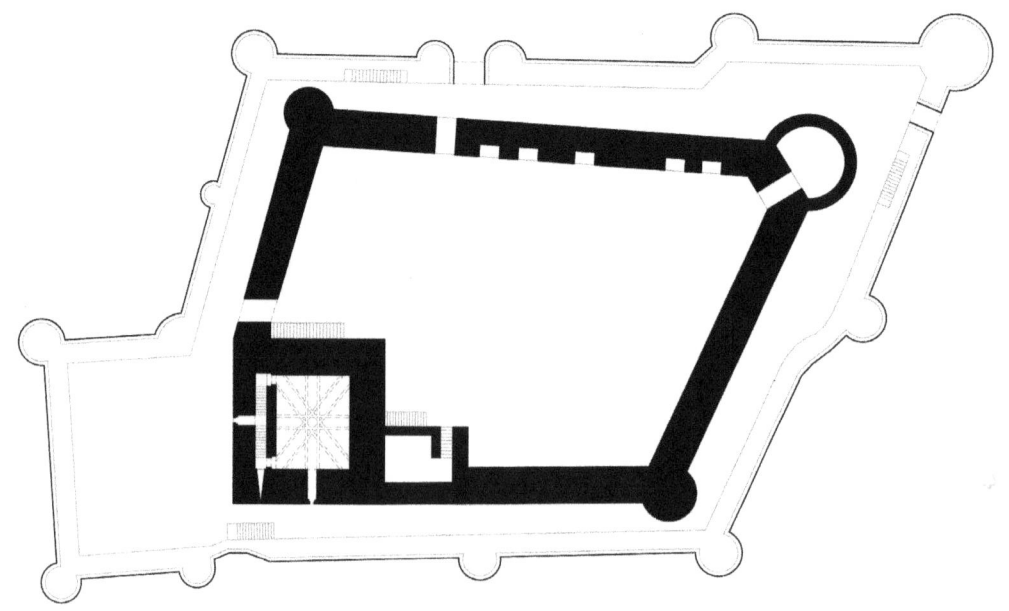

Villena Castle, Alicante, Spain

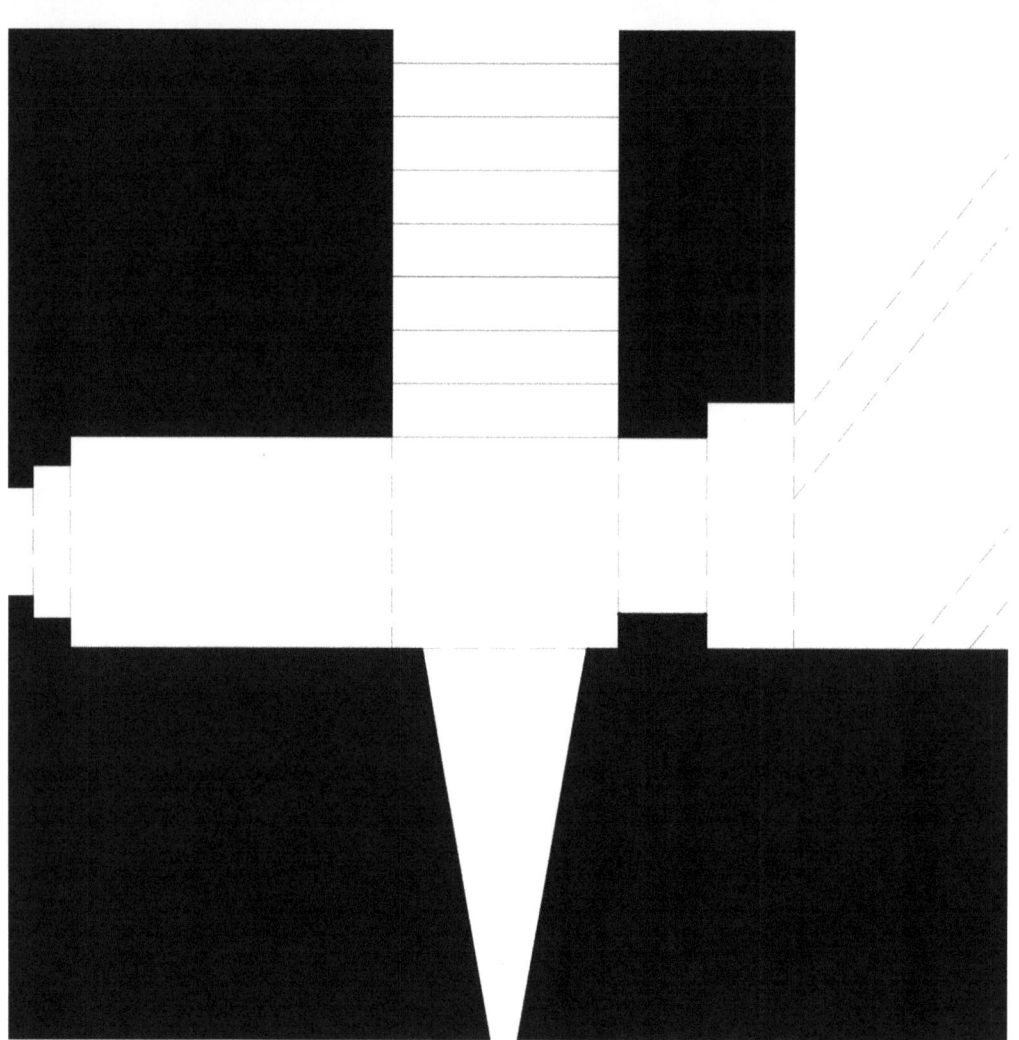

Villena Castle, Alicante, Spain

39.563817, 2.619319

Situated atop the pinnacle of Palma, located within Mallorca, Spain, lies Bellver Castle. Built by Pere Salvá in the 14th century primarily in the catalonian gothic-style, the round nature of this citadel is atypical. Surrounding the two tiered central courtyard are three defence towers and a tall free-standing keep that is linked to the main castle by a small bridge. Originally designed as a palace for royal residences under rule of King James II, it was converted into a military prison in the 18th century.

Rooted within the landscape, Bellver's radial form unfolds like a stone blossom, its circular geometry emblematic of military advancements of fortification. Encircled by dense forestry, it emerges as if sculpted by the land itself, appearing to be naturally grown and harmonizing with the terrain. The courtyard is framed by a rhythmic colonnade, its arches forming a skeletal embrace that binds the structure together. The organic framework, both delicate and unyielding, breathes life into the fortress, softening its defensive purpose into something almost serene. Here ingenuity dissolves into elegance, the castle stands not just as a stronghold, but as a quiet echo of the past.

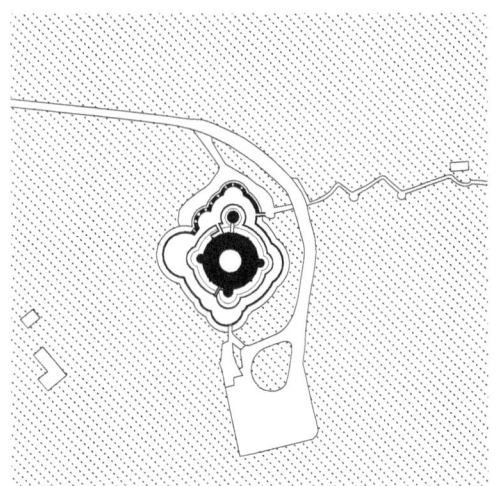
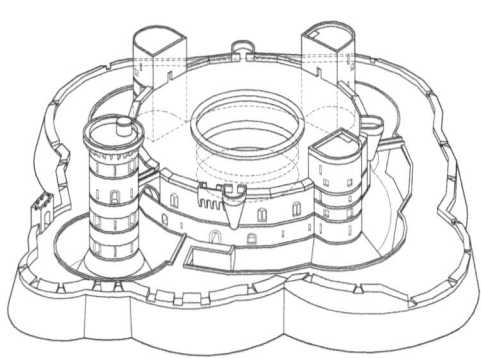

Bellver Castle, Mallorca, Spain

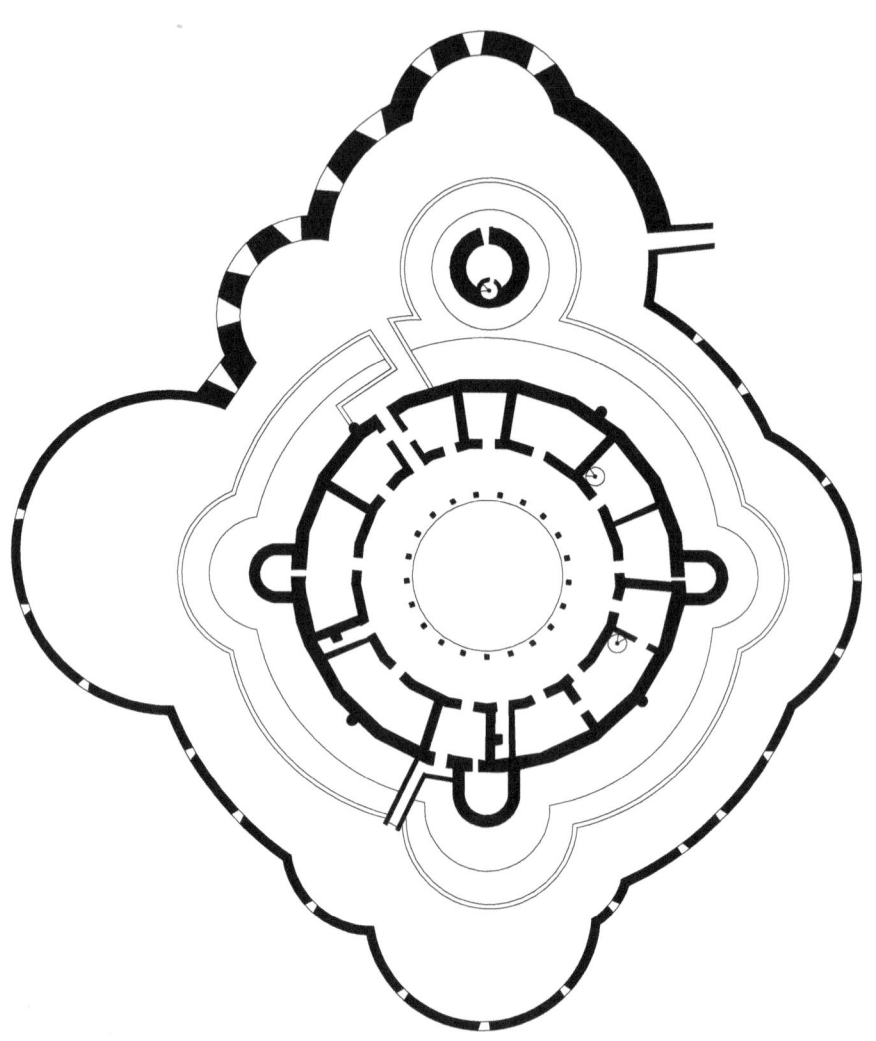

Architectural Precedents | Historic Case Studies

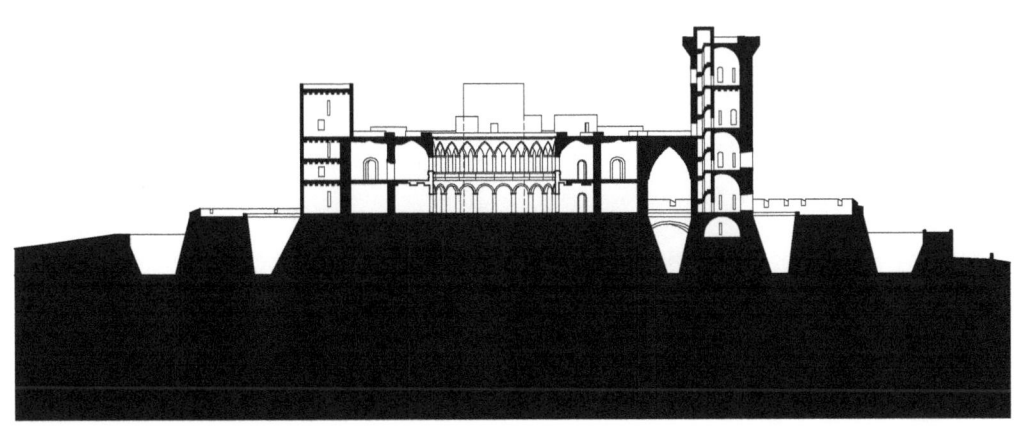

Bellver Castle, Mallorca, Spain   125

Architectural Precedents | Historic Case Studies

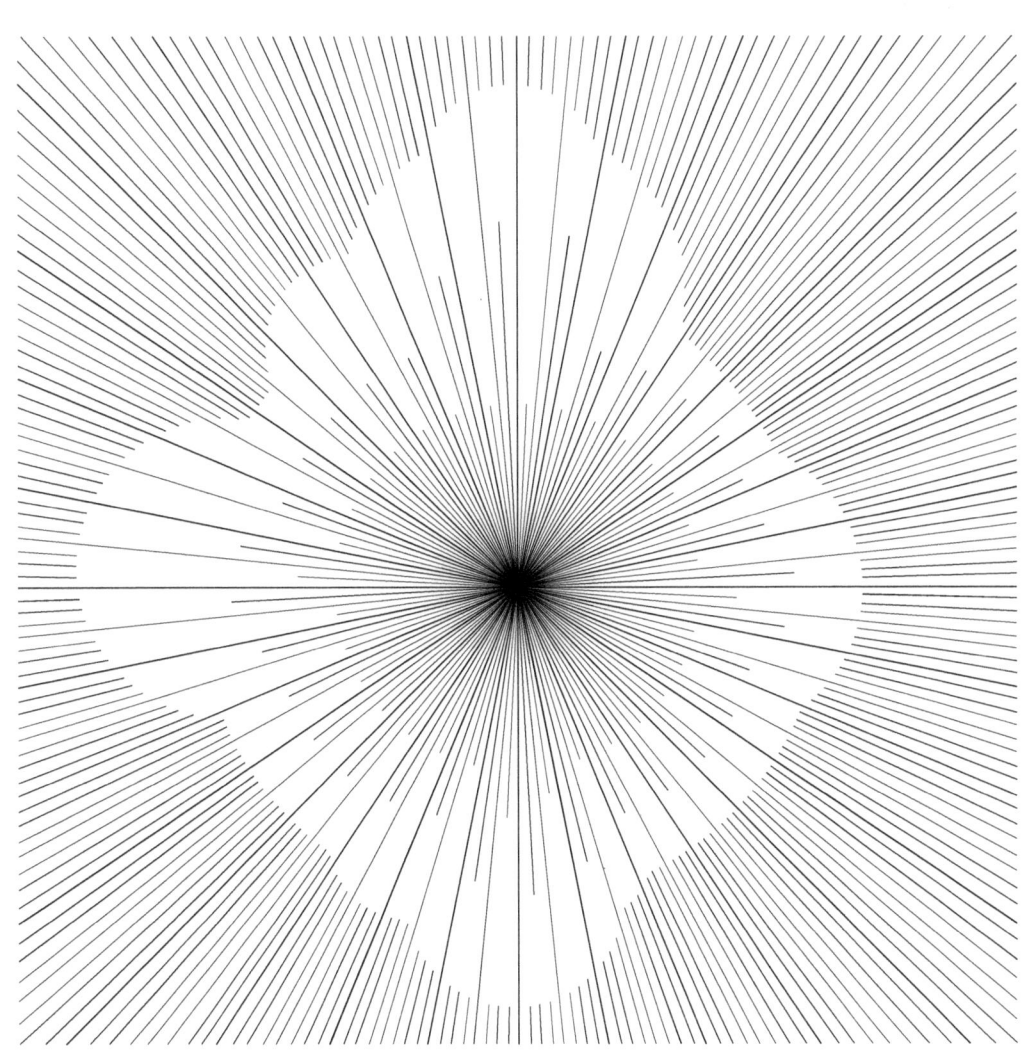

Bellver Castle, Mallorca, Spain

Butrón Castle
Vizcaya, Spain

Abandoned, waiting patiently on a hill in Vizcaya, Spain, this 14th century gothic-style castle was originally under rule of the Butrón dynasty in the 8th century, considered then to be more of a Tower house. It was host to a series of wars, leaving it to erode and deteriorate. Francisco de Cubas was tasked in its restoration transforming the structure into a more fantastical medieval-style castle that still stands to this day. The floor plan is marked by four prominent bastions that contrast sharply with the keep and facade.

Glimpses of a palimpsest of textures weave through the castle's weathered stone, each surface inscribed with the passage of time, whispering stories that shape its character. This castle does not stand as a fortress of war, it culminates here as a fairytale pilgrimage through dense forestry. Designed not for defense but as a spectacle, its architecture resonates with a light-handed symmetry. Its form balanced, yet untamed, the harsh jagged edges softened by nature's embrace. The four outer towers, meant to frame its perimeter, are eclipsed by the commanding central mass. This structure does not impose itself upon the landscape, it rests eternally here, waiting to be discovered.

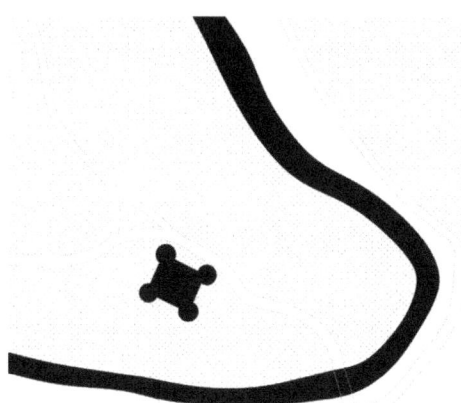

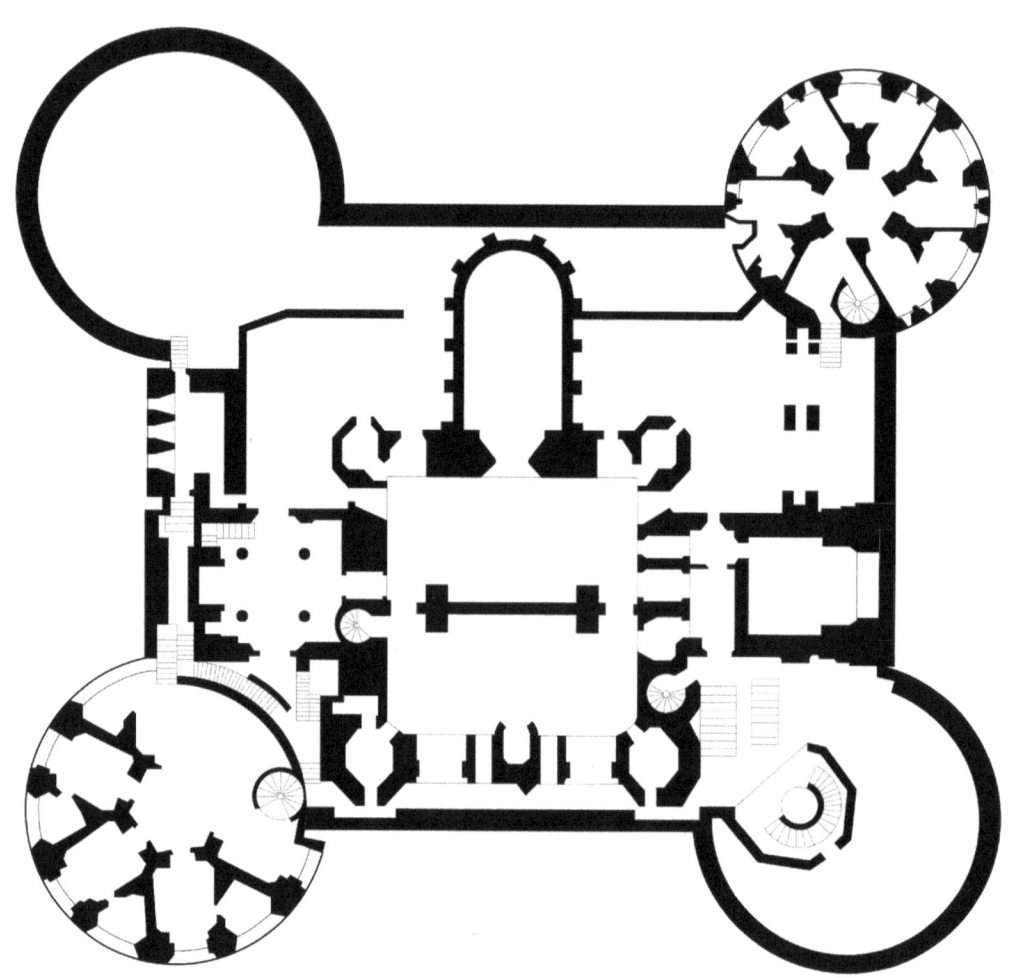

Architectural Precedents | Historic Case Studies

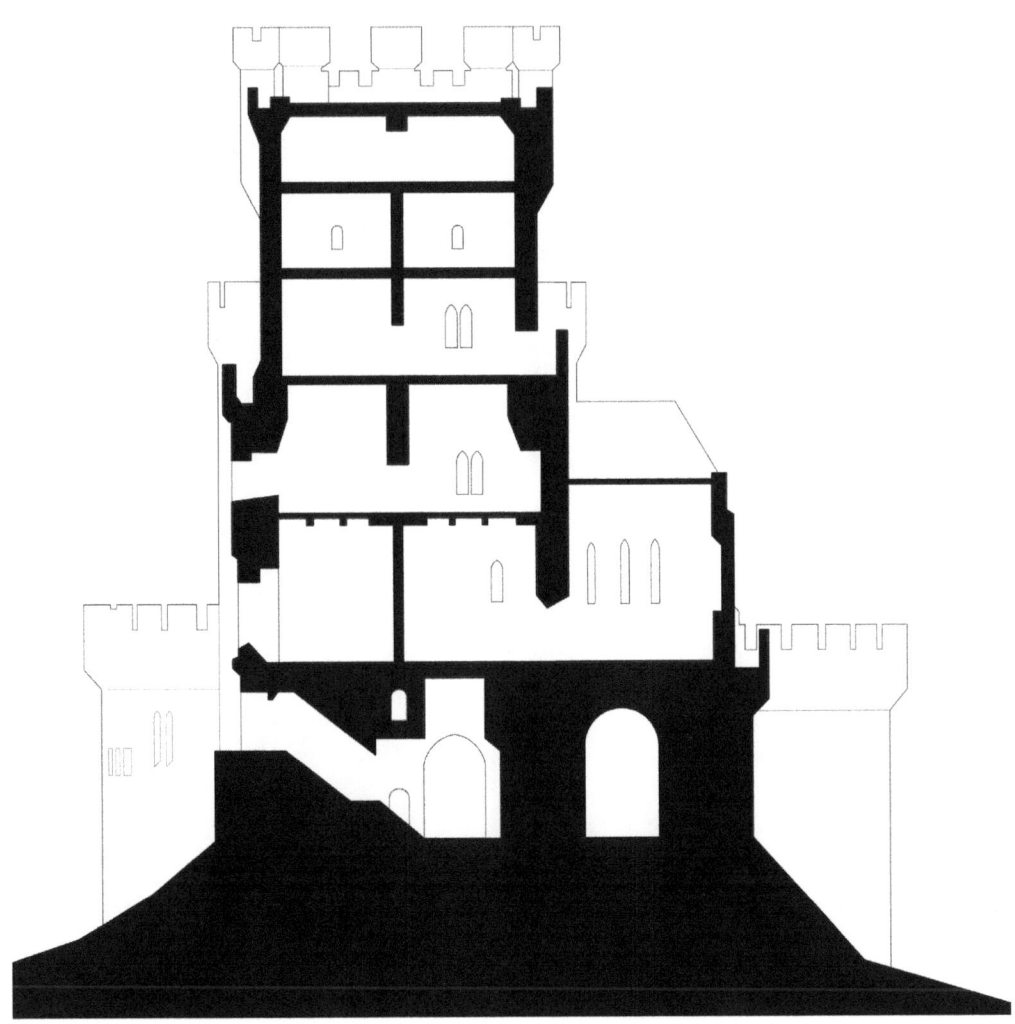

Butrón Castle, Vizcaya, Spain 131

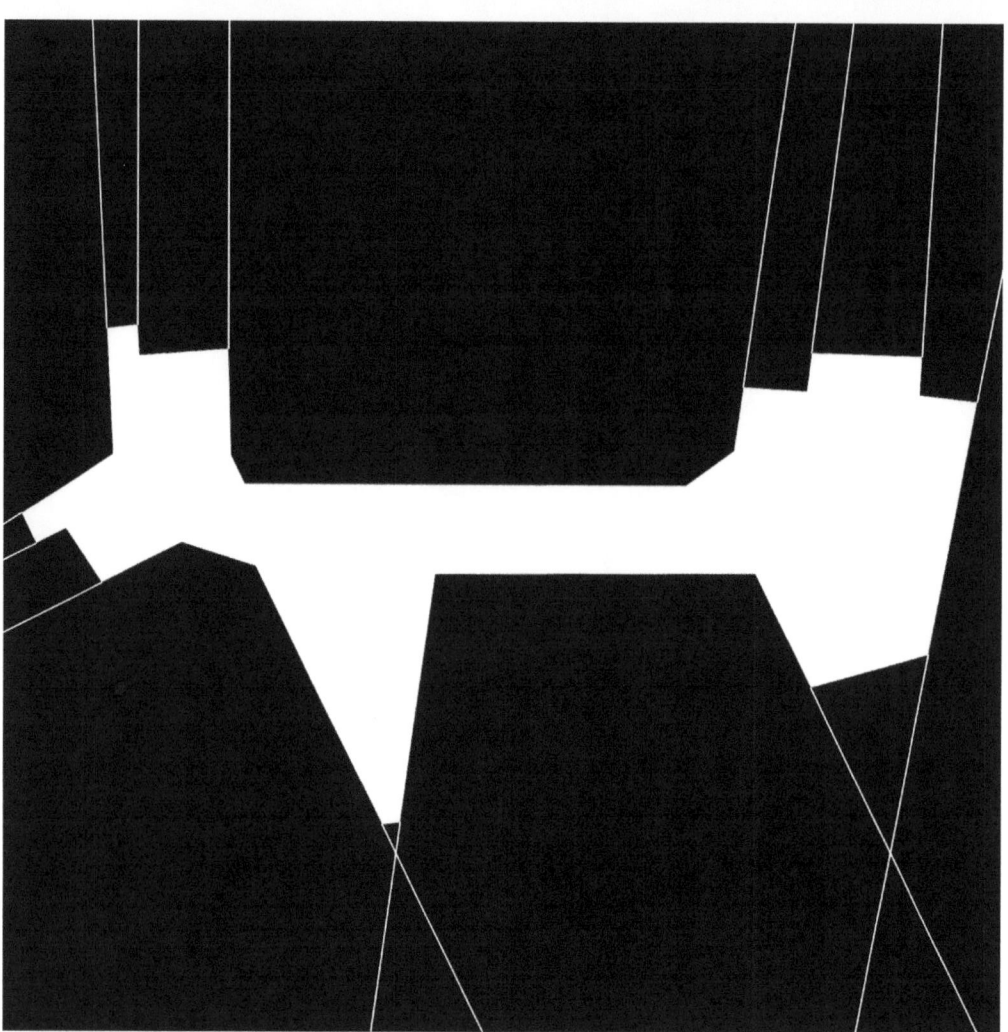

Architectural Precedents | Historic Case Studies

Butrón Castle, Vizcaya, Spain

41.215167, -4.525515

Coca Castle
Segovia, Spain

Placed atop the flat plains of Coca, this castle embodies the mixture of western and Moorish military architecture. Built by the Archbishop of Seville and Don Alonso de Fonseca during the Revolt of the Comuneros, this 15th century structure is made up of two square baileys along with machicolated walls and corner towers. Coca Castle is primarily composed of a brick assembly that has been laid on a smooth surface, allowing the mortar layers and lines to be emphasized as a decorative surface pattern.

Emerging as if sculpted from the earth itself, the castle's walls and towers taper downward, their forms dissolving into the ground in a seamless exchange between architecture and landscape. Each tier of ornamentation unfurls like exposed strata, as if the very layers of the land had been drawn upward into its facade, solidifying into a splendor tapestry of brick and stone. From its core, dense rectilinear bastions radiate outward, their rhythmic massing a testament to impenetrability. Yet, despite its defensive might, the castle possesses an organic synthesis of fortification and artistry, where strength and embellishment entwine, rooted in the land yet reaching toward the sky.

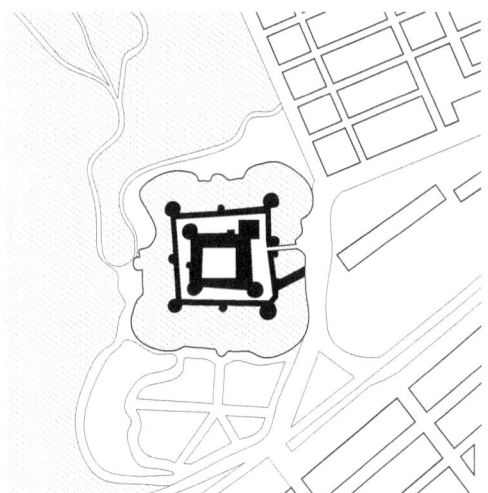
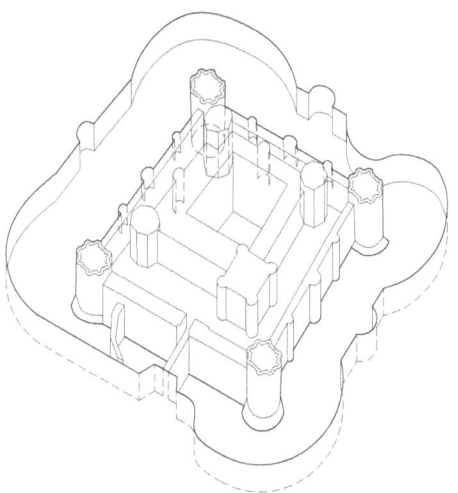

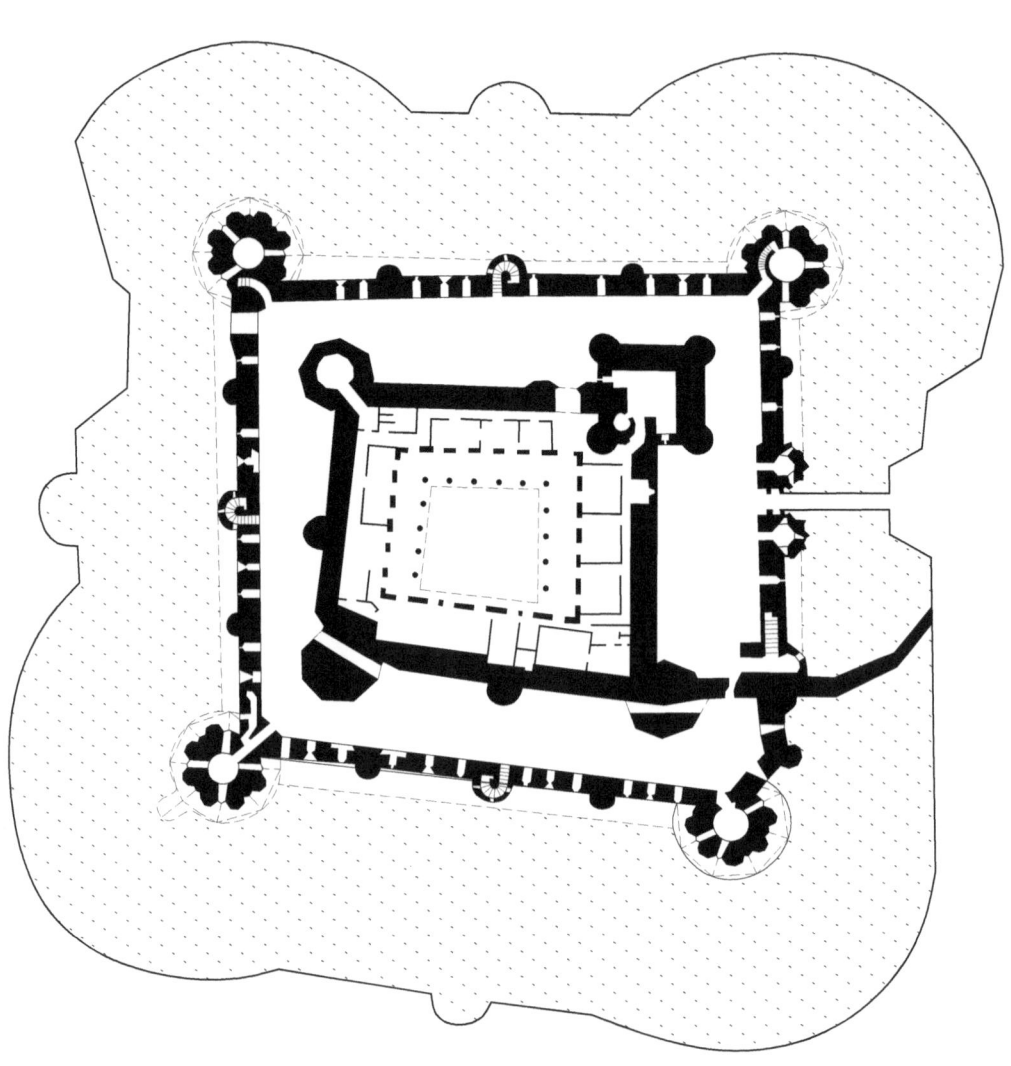

Architectural Precedents | Historic Case Studies

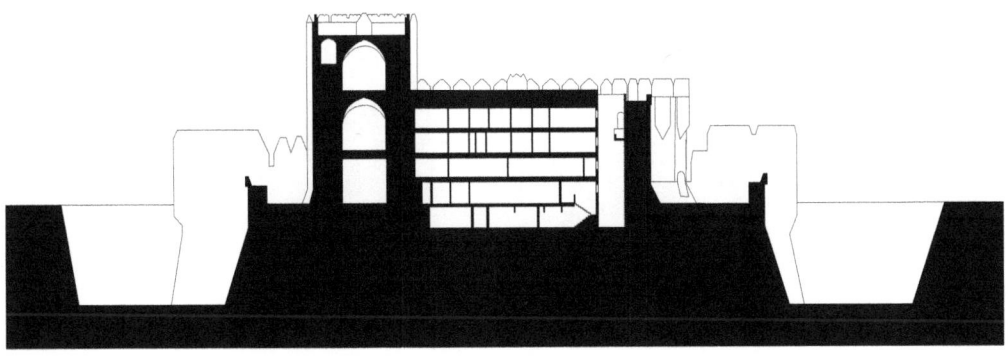

Coca Castle, Segovia, Spain

Architectural Precedents | Historic Case Studies

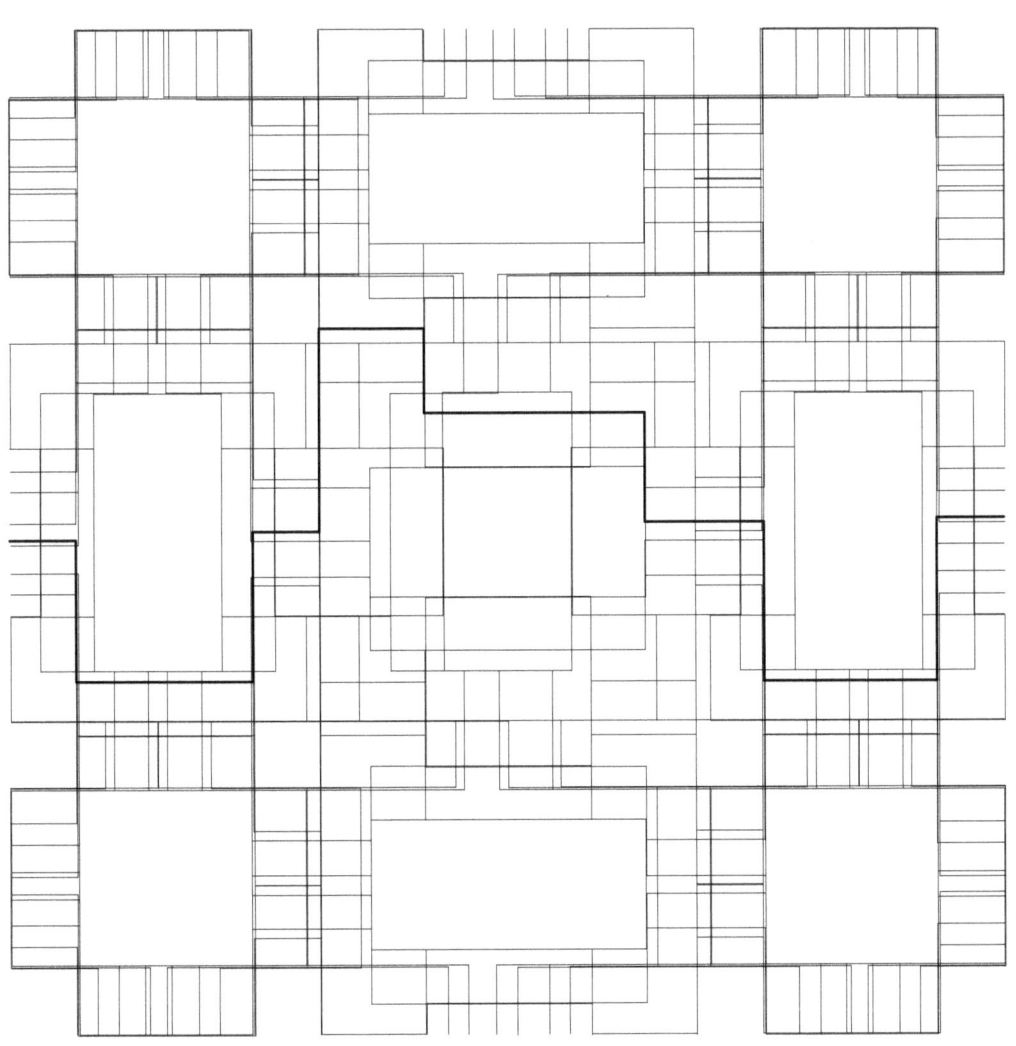

Coca Castle, Segovia, Spain

Belmonte Castle
Cuenca, Spain

Rising from the gentle Cerro de San Cristobal, this one story Gothic-Mudejar castle was built in the second half of the 15th century by order of Don Juan Pacheco. Its plan follows an equilateral triangle, forming a six-pointed star reinforced by six cylindrical towers, each approximately 22 meters tall. Constructed primarily from ashlar masonry, the structure is protected by a surrounding artillery barrier. The castle houses Mudejar coffered ceilings, polychrome muqarnas, and detailed woodwork.

The presence of Belmonte is defined by its geometric clarity and internal coherence. The acute triangular plan, extruded into a star shaped configuration, organizes space through axial precision and mirrored balance. Each tower operates as an anchor, reinforcing the perimeter while modulating interior scale. Circulation follows the logic of this geometry, with stepped galleries and corner transitions aligning movement to structure. Ornament serves to articulate shifts in program and status, rather than act as surface decoration. The castle's strength lies not in vertical dominance, but in its deliberate spatial rhythm and formal restraint.

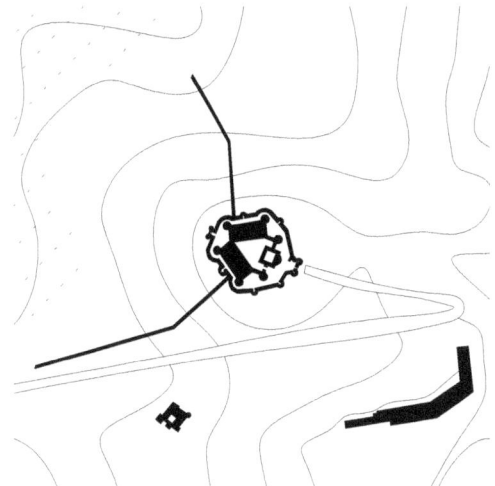
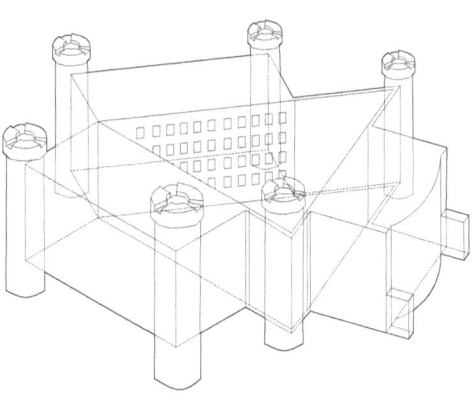

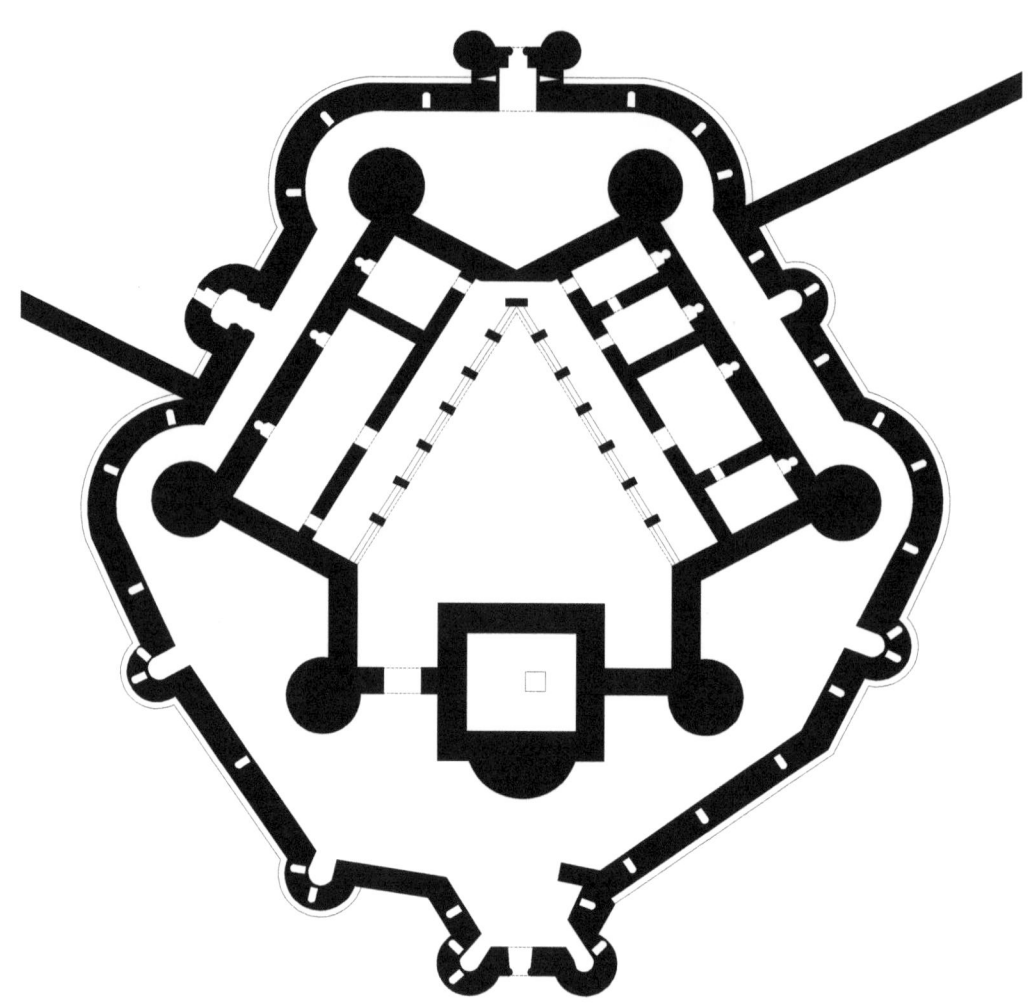

Architectural Precedents | Historic Case Studies

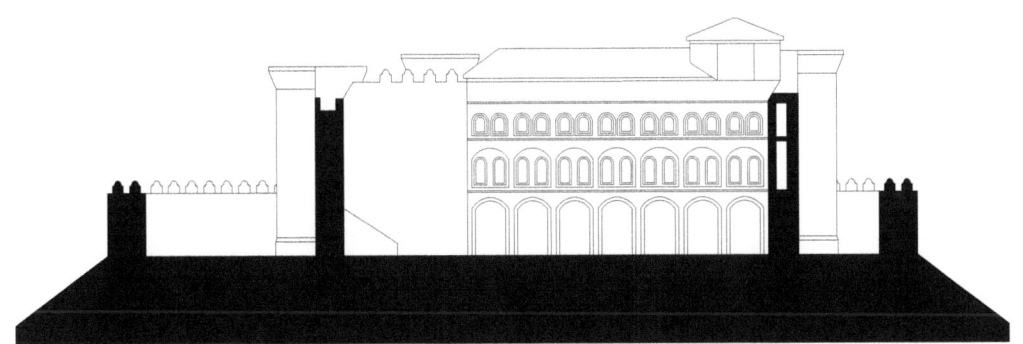

Belmonte Castle, Cuenca, Spain   143

Architectural Precedents | Historic Case Studies

Construction began in the 15th century by Diego Hurtado de Mendoza, and it was finished by the first Marquis of Santillana, Íñigo López de Mendoza. Containing a central square floor plan, the plan expands into a series of round towers at the corners and a polygonal keep. The castle consists of a courtyard, a basement, and six floors. This castle is an example of Isabelline Gothic and Castilian military architecture, its defensive structures contrast with the delicacy of its palatial galleries and viewing points.

Anchored on a hill overlooking the mountains, this castle rises with a sculpted precision, its rectilinear form crowned by elegant cylindrical towers, each adorned with delicate gothic flourishes. The stone, hewn from the surrounding land, bears the golden hues of the landscape, its warm textures shifting with the light as if echoing the movement of time itself. A fusion of military strength and aristocratic refinement, its crenellations and machicolations whisper of defense, inviting the eye to linger. The castle is not just a fortress but a statement, an architectural testament to power, prestige, and the timeless dance between protection and beauty.

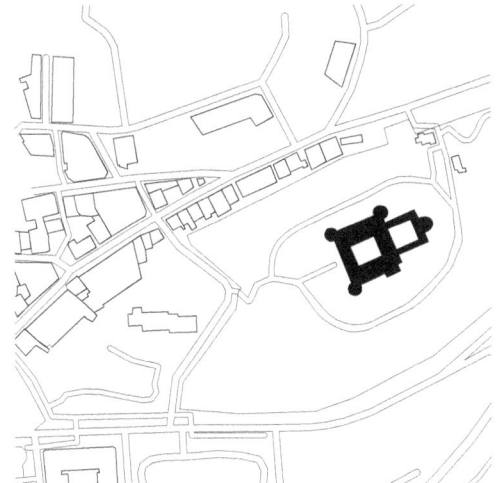
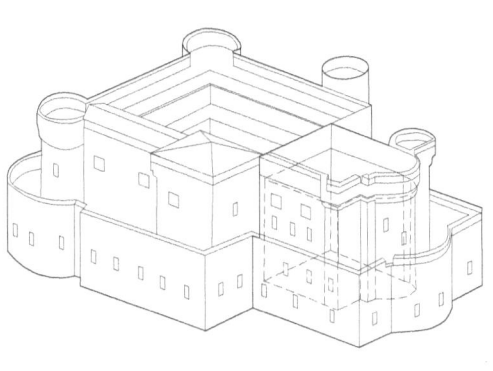

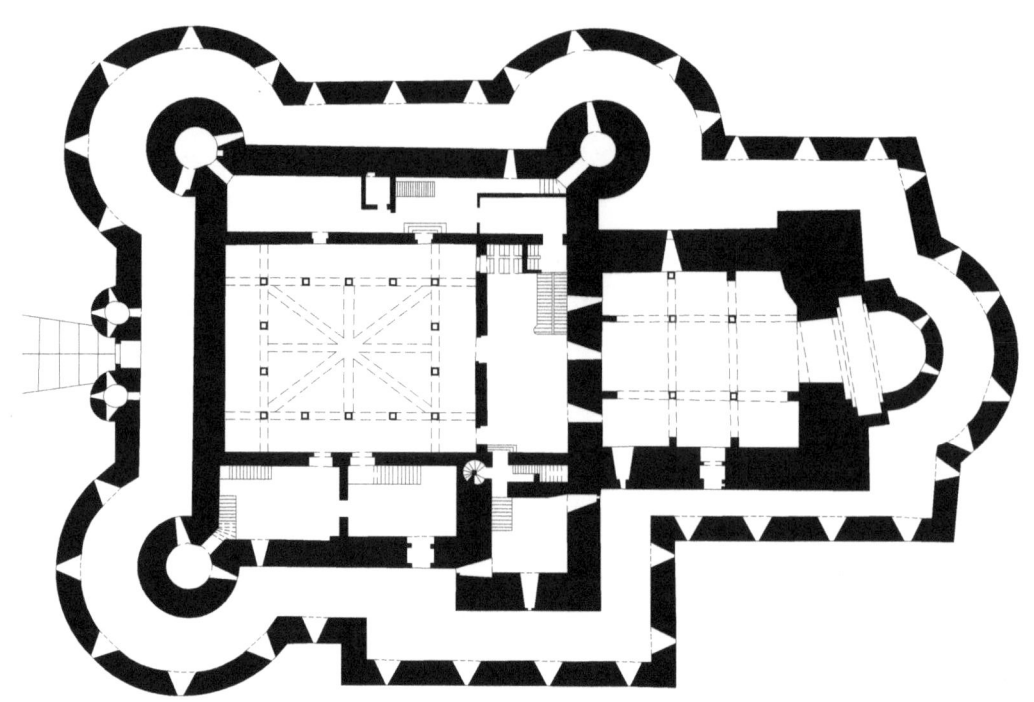

Manzanares El Real Castle, Madrid, Spain 149

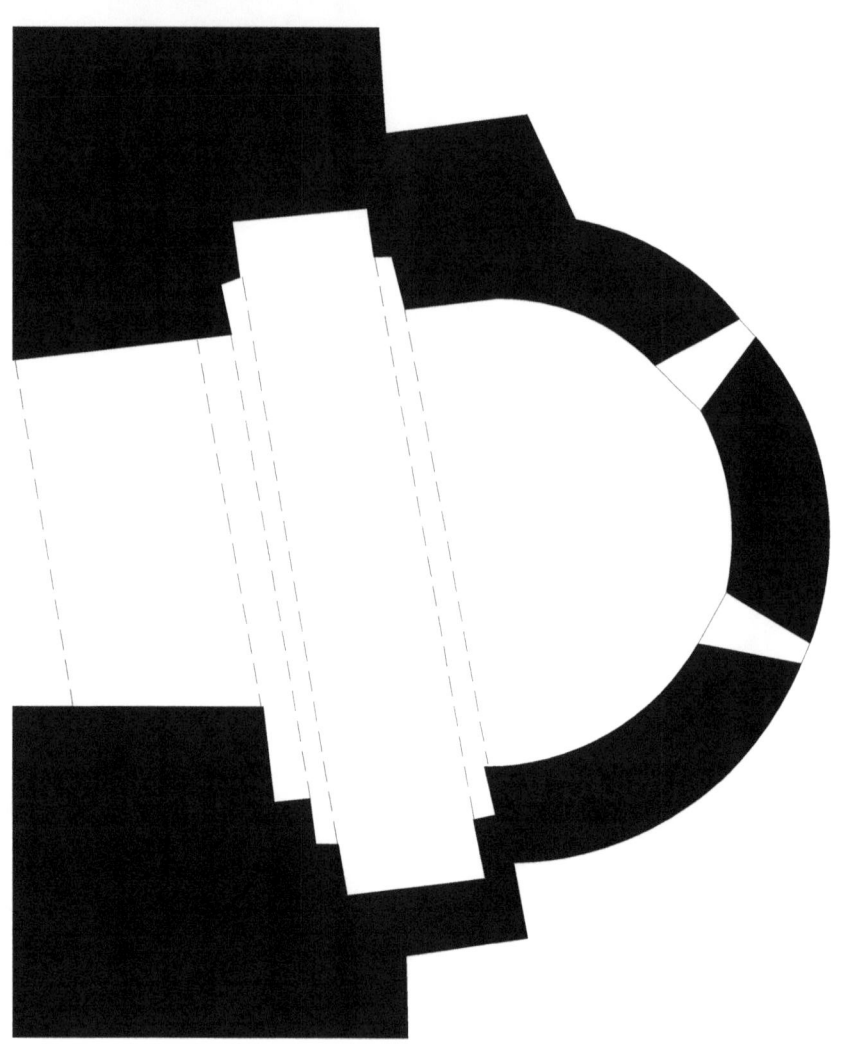

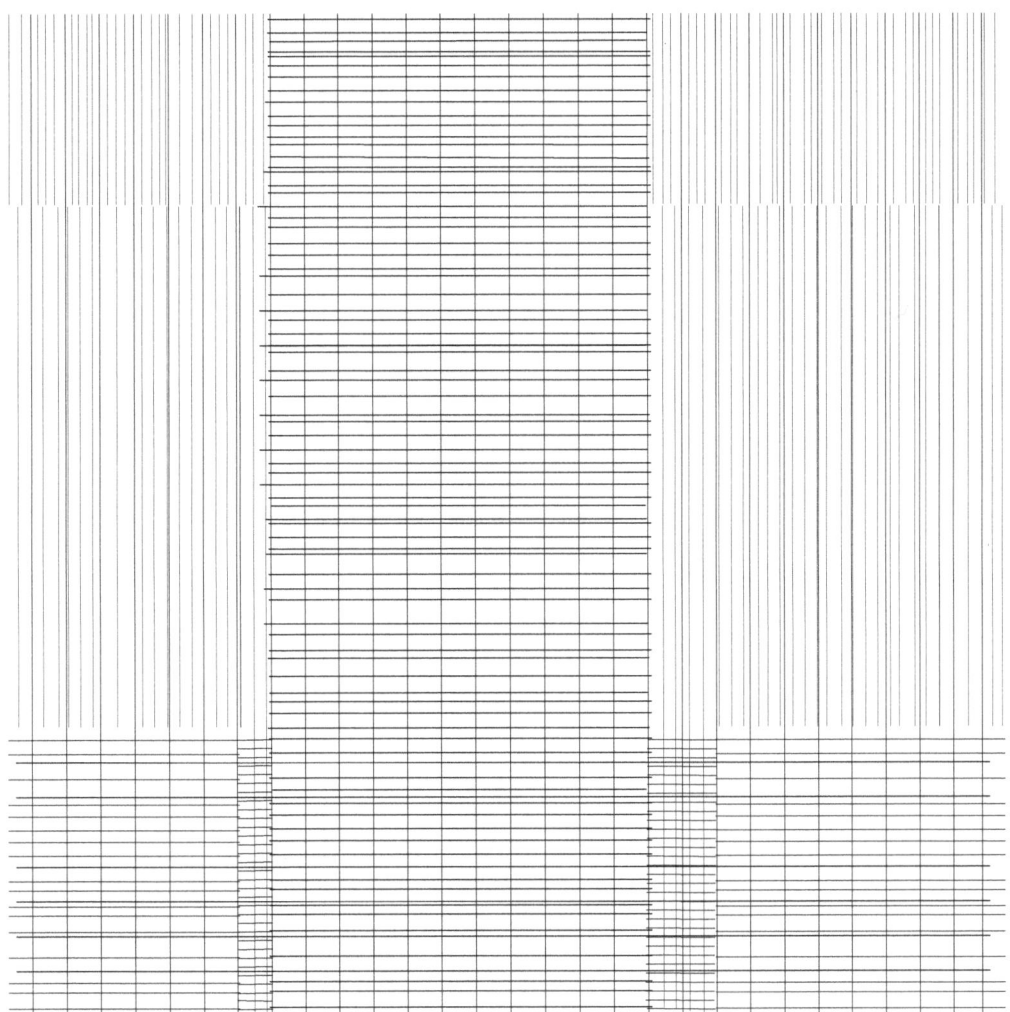

Manzanares El Real Castle, Madrid, Spain

Belalcázar Castle
Córdoba, Spain

A striking example of Gothic military architecture, Belalcázar was built in the 15th century under Gutierre de Sotomayor, Master of the Order of Alcántara. Rising 47 meters, its Torre del Homenaje is the tallest keep in Spain, dominating the landscape of northern Córdoba. The cuboid fortress, constructed from granite ashlar, is flanked by eight prism shaped towers. In 1539 Hernán Ruiz I added a Renaissance Palace. Despite its resilience, the castle suffered damage during the Peninsular War.

A fortress that reaches towards the sky, commanding its surroundings. The colossal keep soars above the horizon an unwavering sentinel. The Torre del Homenaje is adorned with bartizans and emblazoned with the Sotomayor coat of arms. Light filters through Gothic wIndows, casting long shadows over the remains of a lost palatial grandeur. The courtyard, where knights once gathered, now stands in a quiet ruin, its porticoes and cistern whispering of a life once thriving within. The orientation of the plan shifted by the rising hillside. This structure, a vessel of an older age remains upright, unwavering, and abrupt, worthy of preservation.

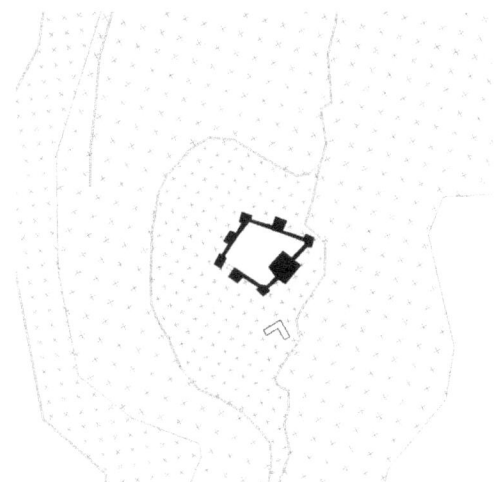
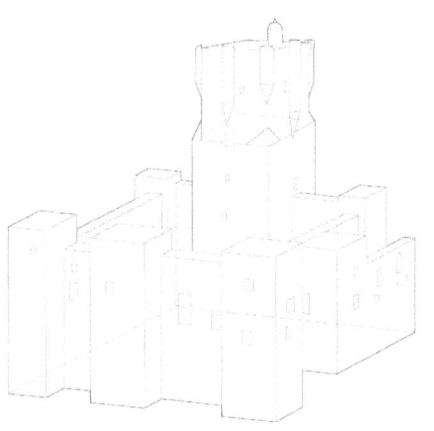

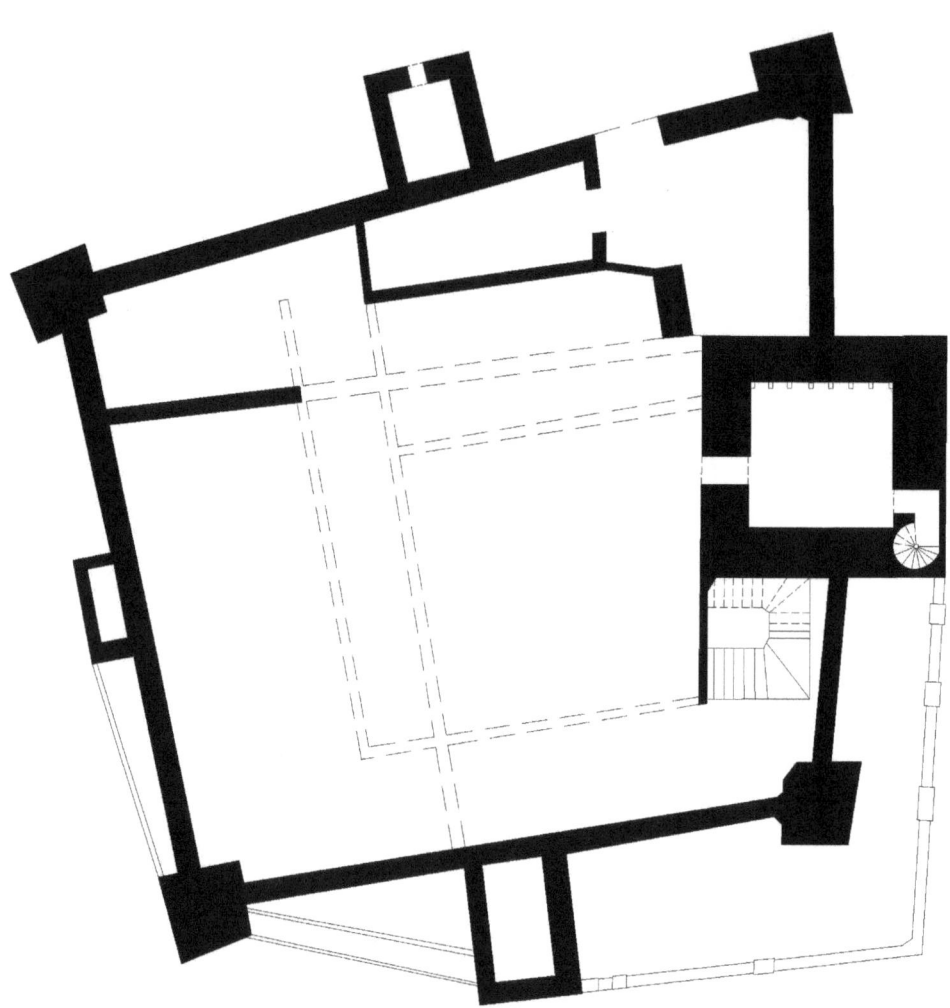

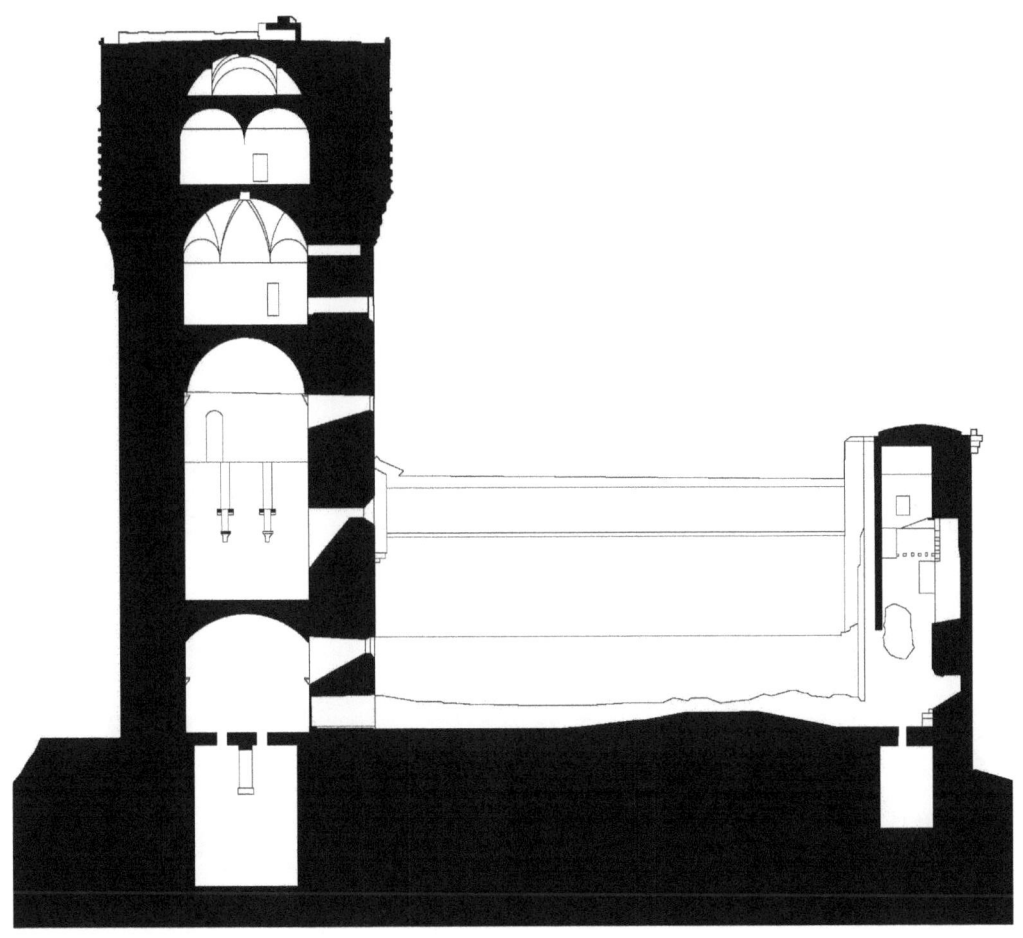

Belalcázar Castle, Córdoba, Spain

155

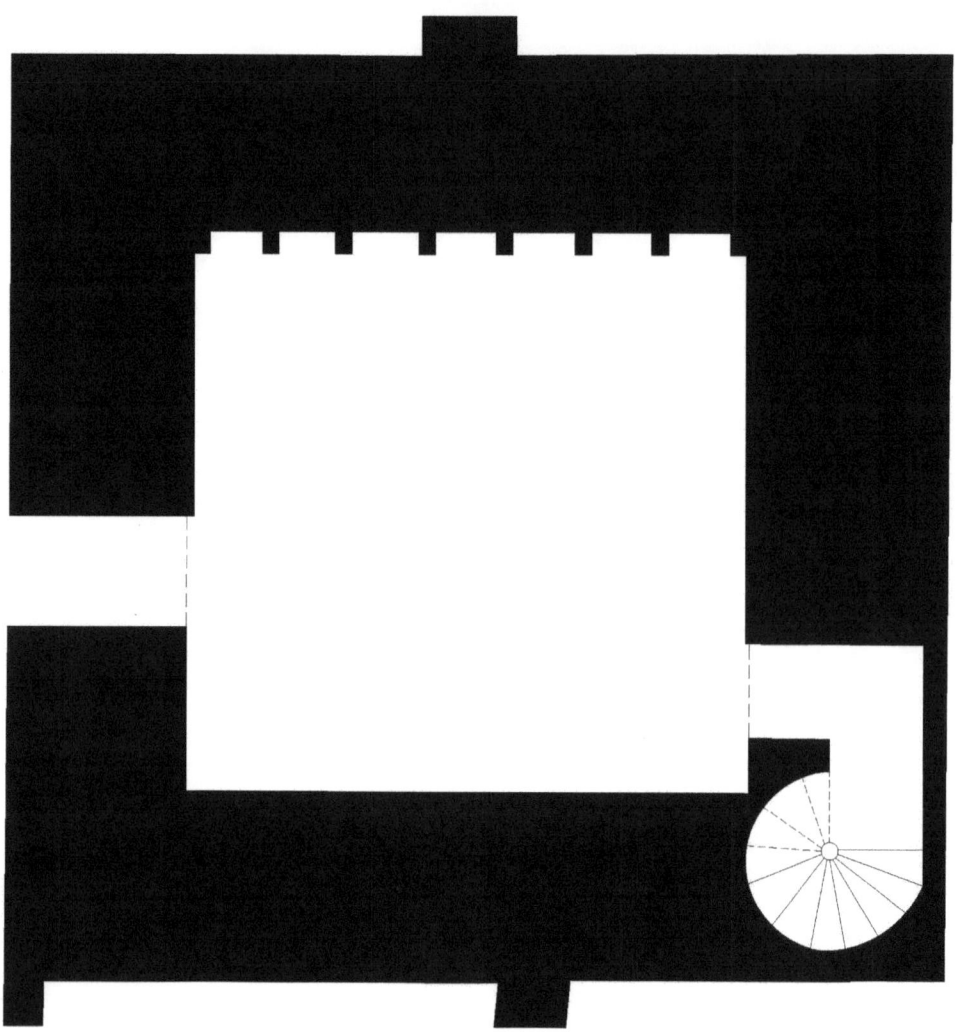

Belalcázar Castle, Córdoba, Spain

Architectural Precedents
Historic Case Studies on Spatial Density and Seclusion

Eastern Monasteries

Sümela Monastery
Karadağ, Turkey

Sümela Monastery is nestled within the Pontic Mountains in the Maçka district of Trabzon Province in modern Turkey, and its founding date has been placed around the 4th century. The complex overlooks the forests below at a high altitude, being necessary to arrive through elevated paths. Some walls are fully covered with frescoes of religious connotations. In addition to its scenic beauty and ancient origins, the monastery serves as a cultural emblem of the region's Byzantine heritage.

The spaces are configured as a very linear sequence, a sort of inhabited thick wall, defining a sharp and clear artificial edge on the side of the mountain. It creates an interior void, where informal volumes appear and adjust to the topography. The scale of the volume towards the valley is manifested with the extensive array of geometric openings, in clear contrast with the irregularities of the rock.

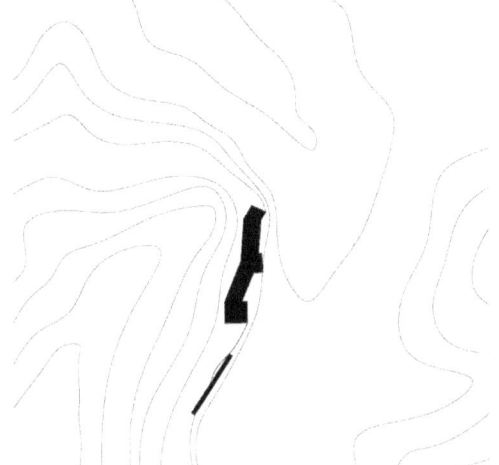

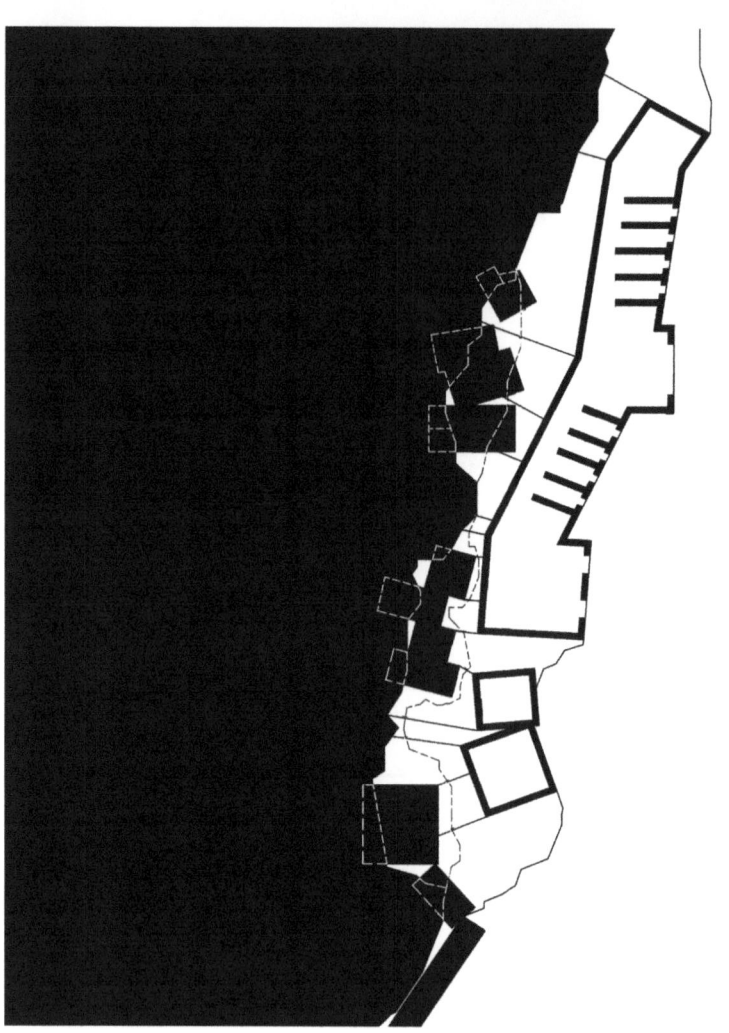

Sümela Monastery, Karadağ, Turkey

Sümela Monastery, Karadağ, Turkey

Saint Catherine Monastery is located on the Holy Mount Sinai, and is the world's oldest continuously inhabited Christian monastery, dating back to the 4th century. Built by the orders of Justinian I, a Byzantine emperor, to enclose Moses' Burning Bush. It houses a treasured library with icons, paintings, manuscripts, and scrolls. This mountainous area is known to be revered by three different and important religions: Christianity, Islam, and Judaism.

The complex defines a solid and clear geometric boundary, densified with construction. That thick, inhabited and constructed wall leaves several open public spaces which are interconnected by subtle openings and paths, as if carved within the solid mass. The main church is oriented following strictly the traditional canon, but differs from the main axis of the overall structure, generating a rich geometric dialog between center and perimeter.

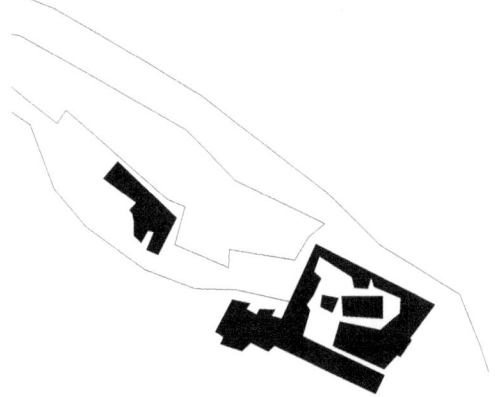
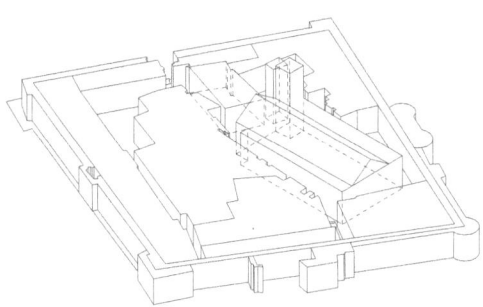

Saint Catherine, South Sinai, Egypt   167

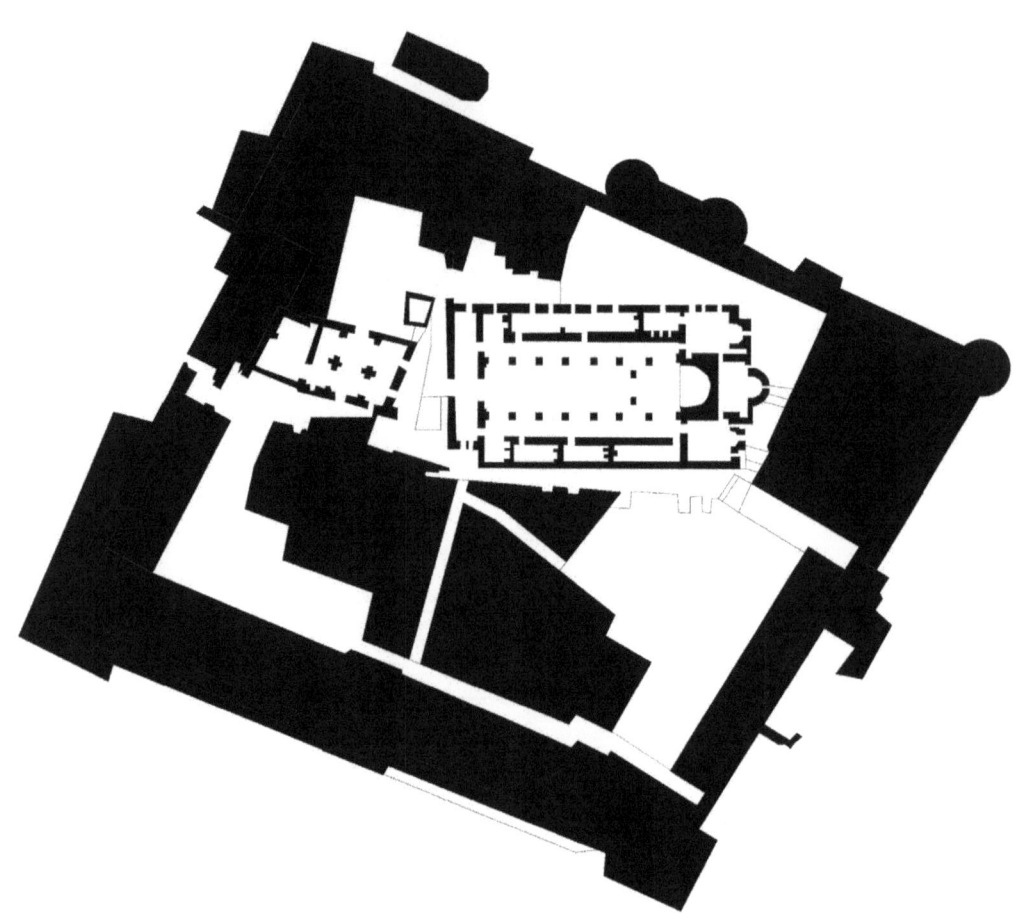

Architectural Precedents | Historic Case Studies

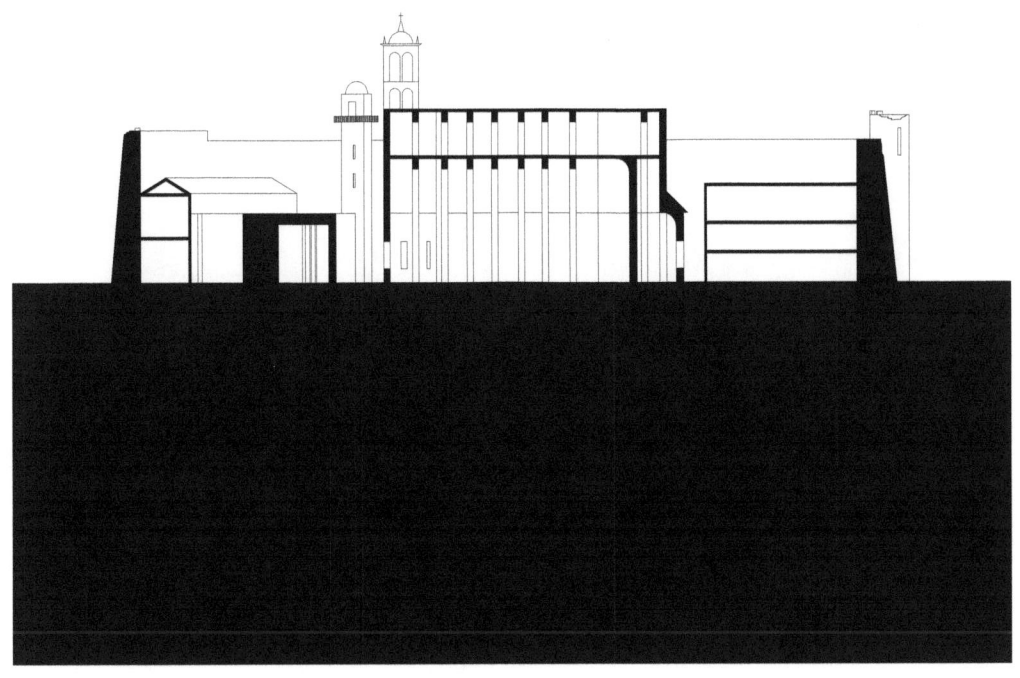

Saint Catherine, South Sinai, Egypt 169

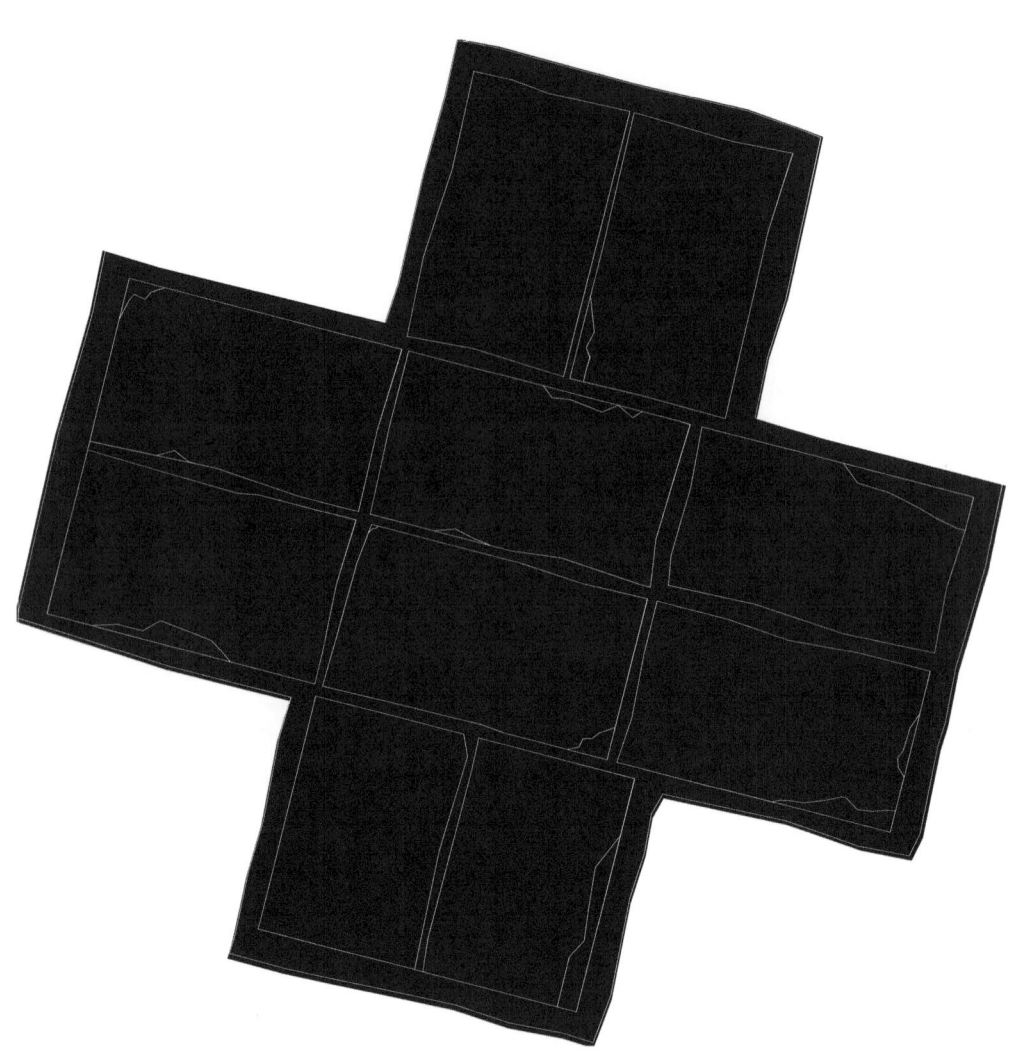

Architectural Precedents | Historic Case Studies

Saint Catherine, South Sinai, Egypt   171

Debre Damo Monastery
Northern Tigray, Ethiopia

Debre Damo Monastery was placed upon an Ethiopian amba, which is a characteristic landform in Ethiopia. Was founded in the 6th century, dating back to Aksumite times. The monastery is only accessible through an arduous rope climb up to the sheer cliff, an expedition that was only given access to men. It was founded by Abba ZeMichael and established by Abuna Aregawi, one of the most revered of the Nine Saints. This fortress preserves some of the oldest illuminated manuscripts of Ethiopia.

Interestingly, the construction expands nearly to the full extent of the plateau, whether using small buildings or by defining marks in the ground with stone walls. Inhabited spaces are clustered, defining nested spaces reacting to different privacy requirements. Retaining and constructed walls have similar nature and geometry, although different materiality and texture.

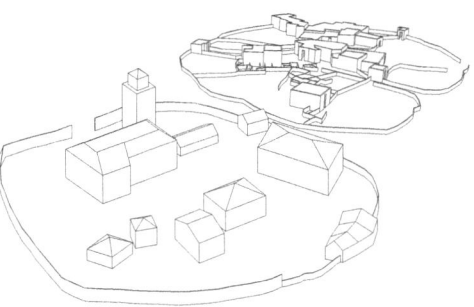

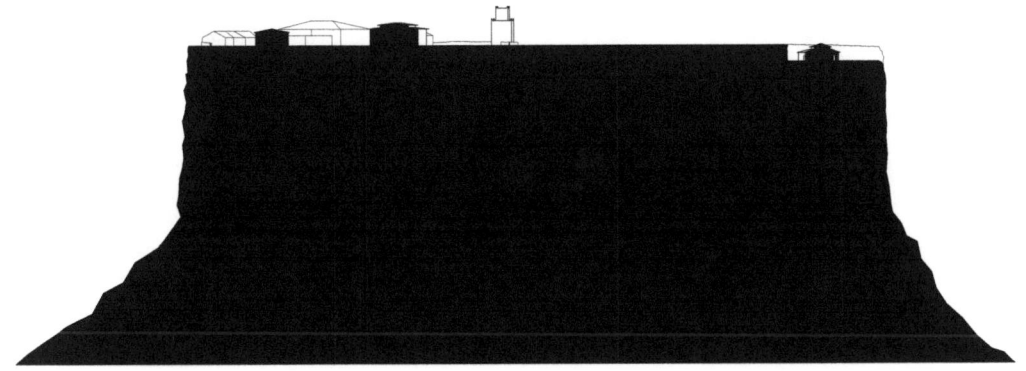

Debre Damo, Northern Tigray, Ethiopia

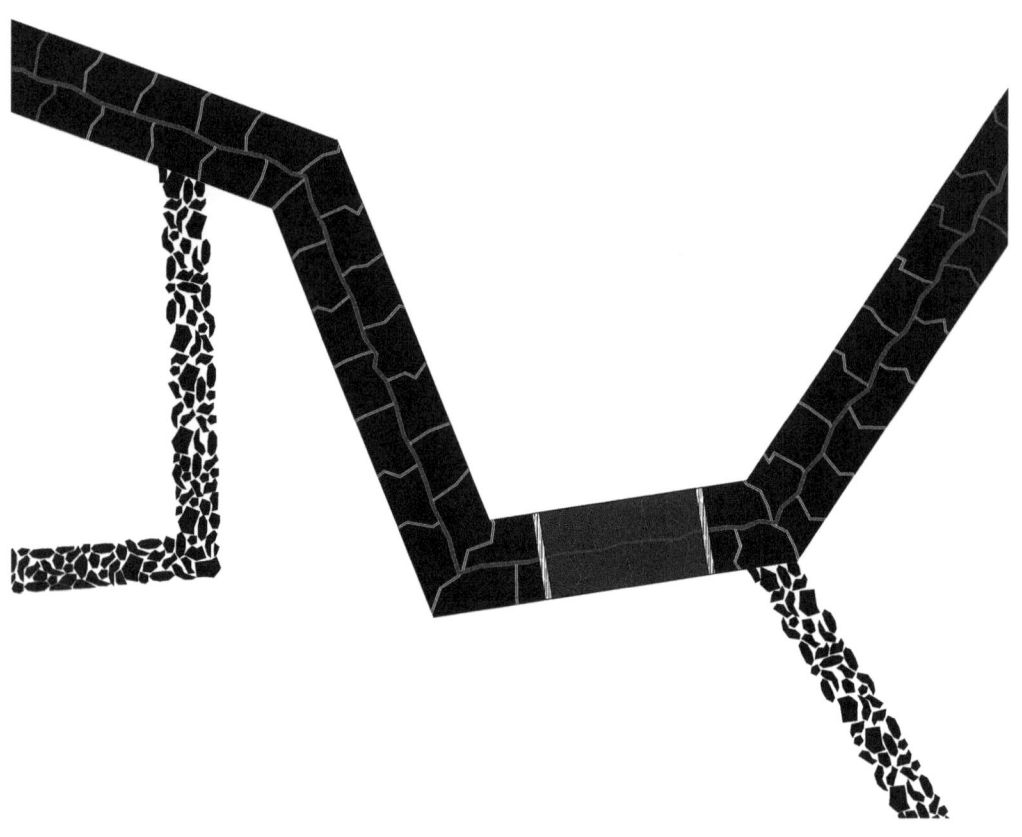

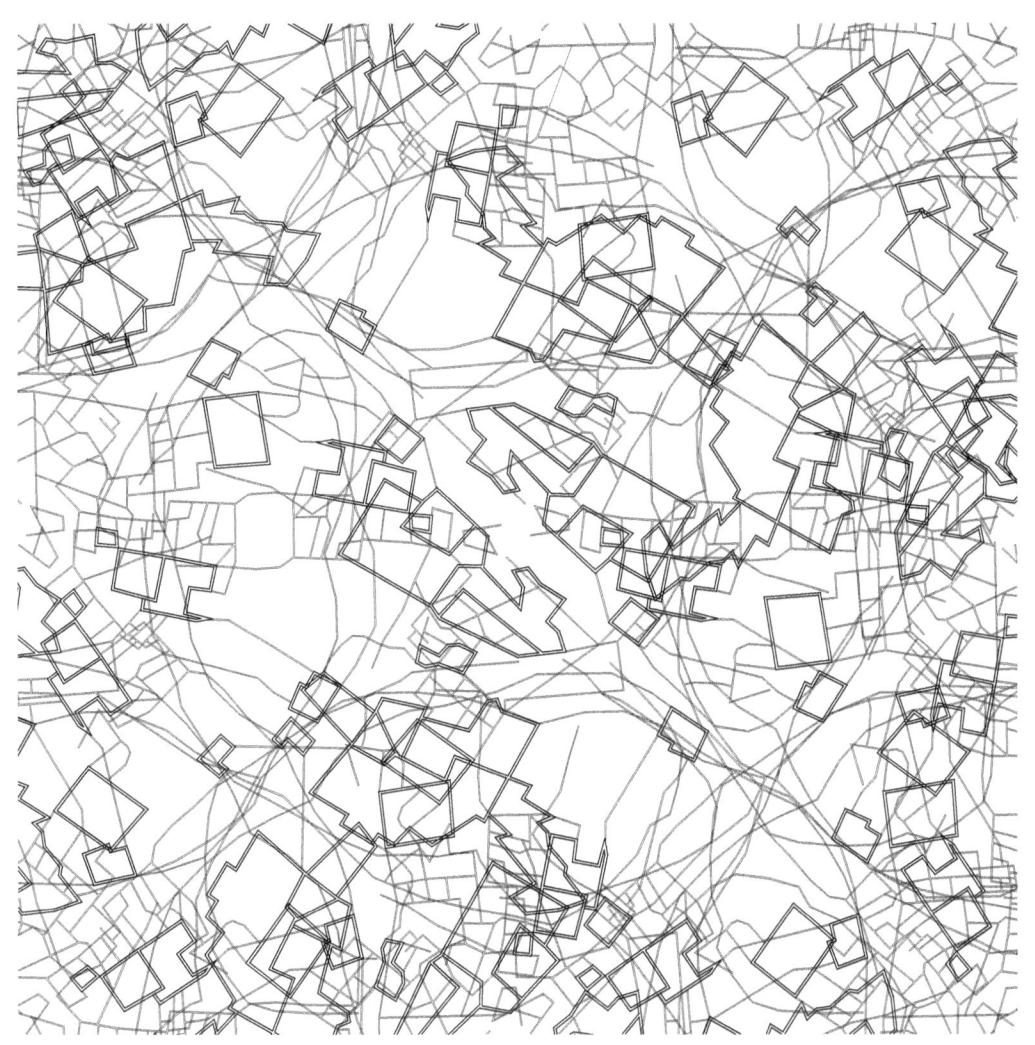

Debre Damo, Northern Tigray, Ethiopia

Tatev Monastery
Syunik, Armenia

Tatev Monastery, named after Eustateus, predominates as a 9th century piece of Armenian Apostolic Christian architecture. Located in a large plateau in South-East Armenia, this monument has played a significant historical role in the region. During the Seljuk invasions and a massive earthquake in the 12th century, the main structure suffered significant damage, eventually being rebuilt. Now it stands as a complex that holds several different programmatic amenities.

Transposed into the terrain is this symmetrically loaded relic of the past, ornamented throughout with religious connotations. Sheltered by the edge of a cascading hillside, occupants are able to flourish in this still active community. The central axis spire serves as a beacon for those who want to make a pilgrimage to this pronounced monastery. This clustered serpentine outpost organization is able to safely open itself up to the rest of the world to share its doctrine.

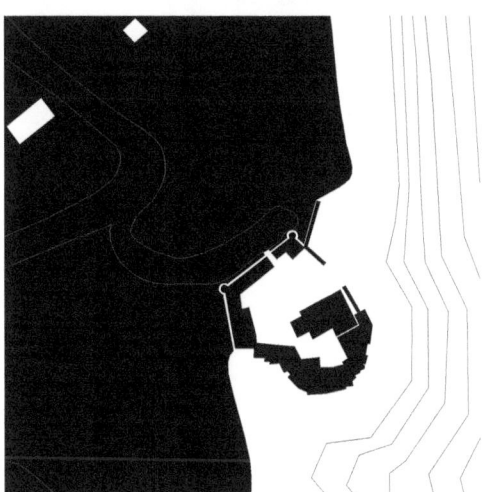
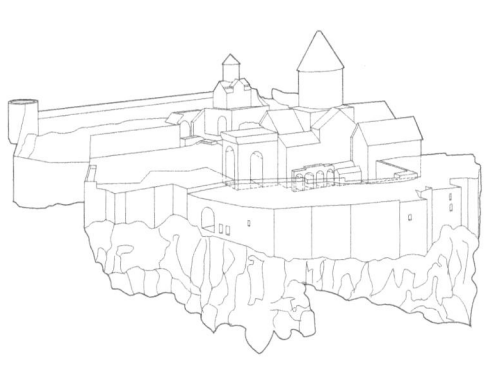

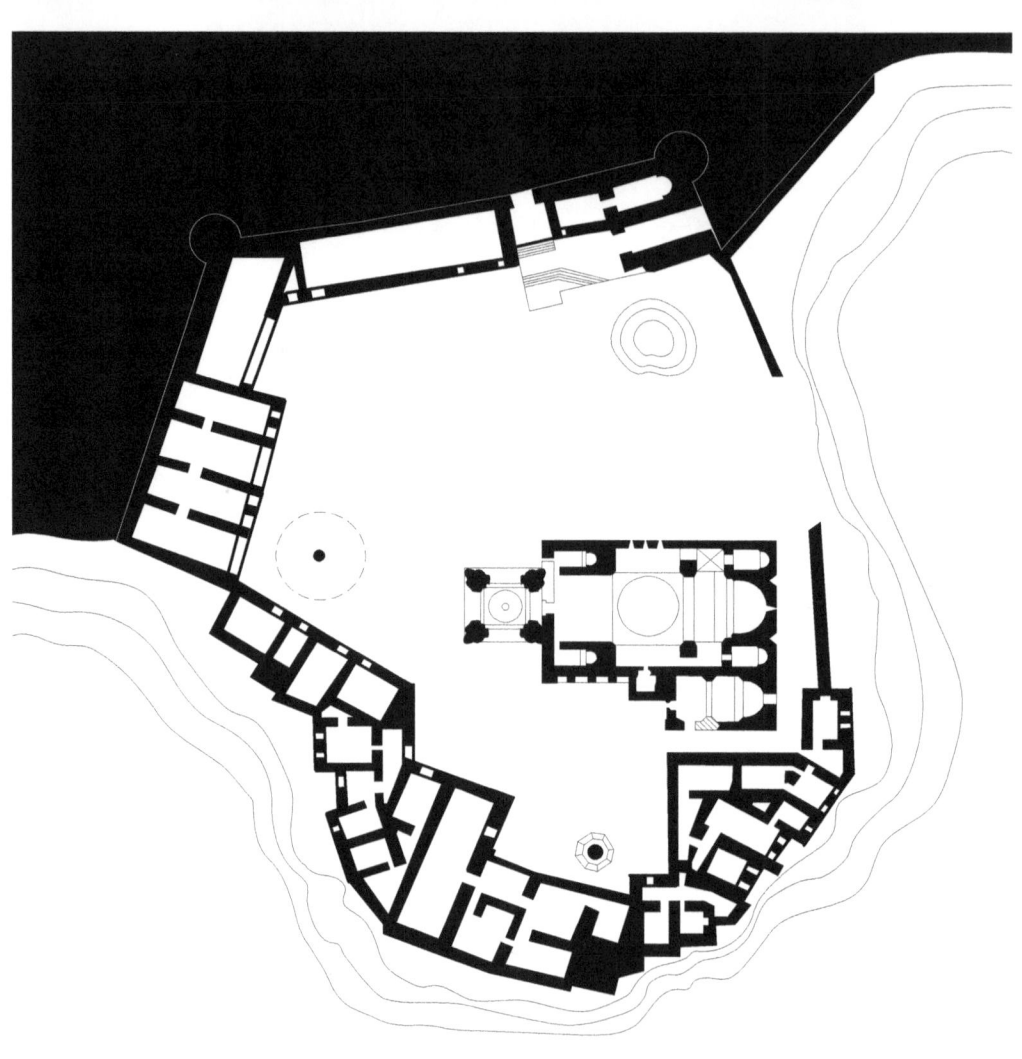

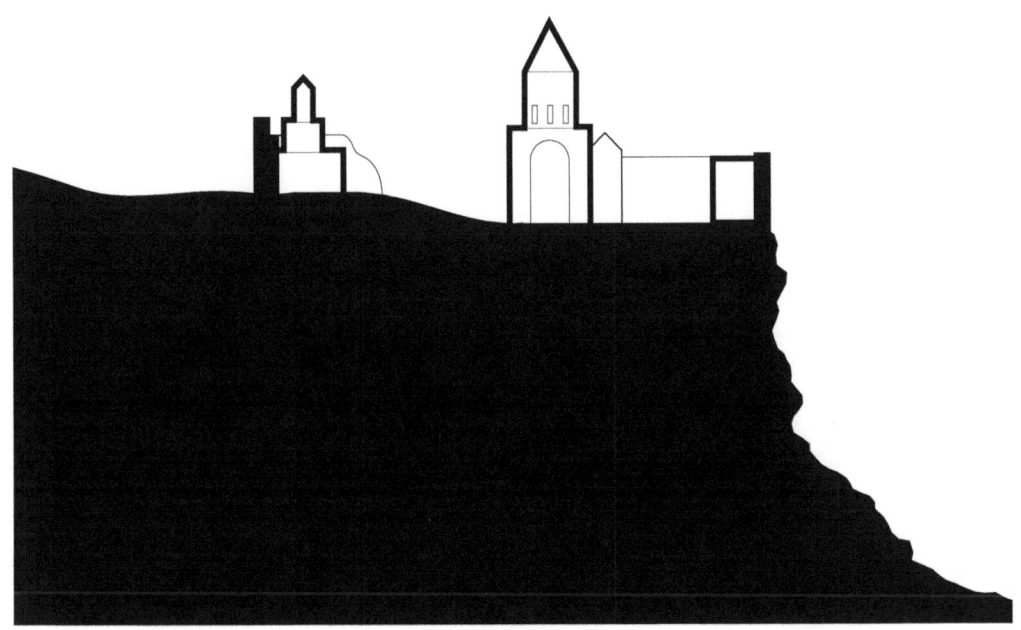

Tatev Monastery, Syunik, Armenia

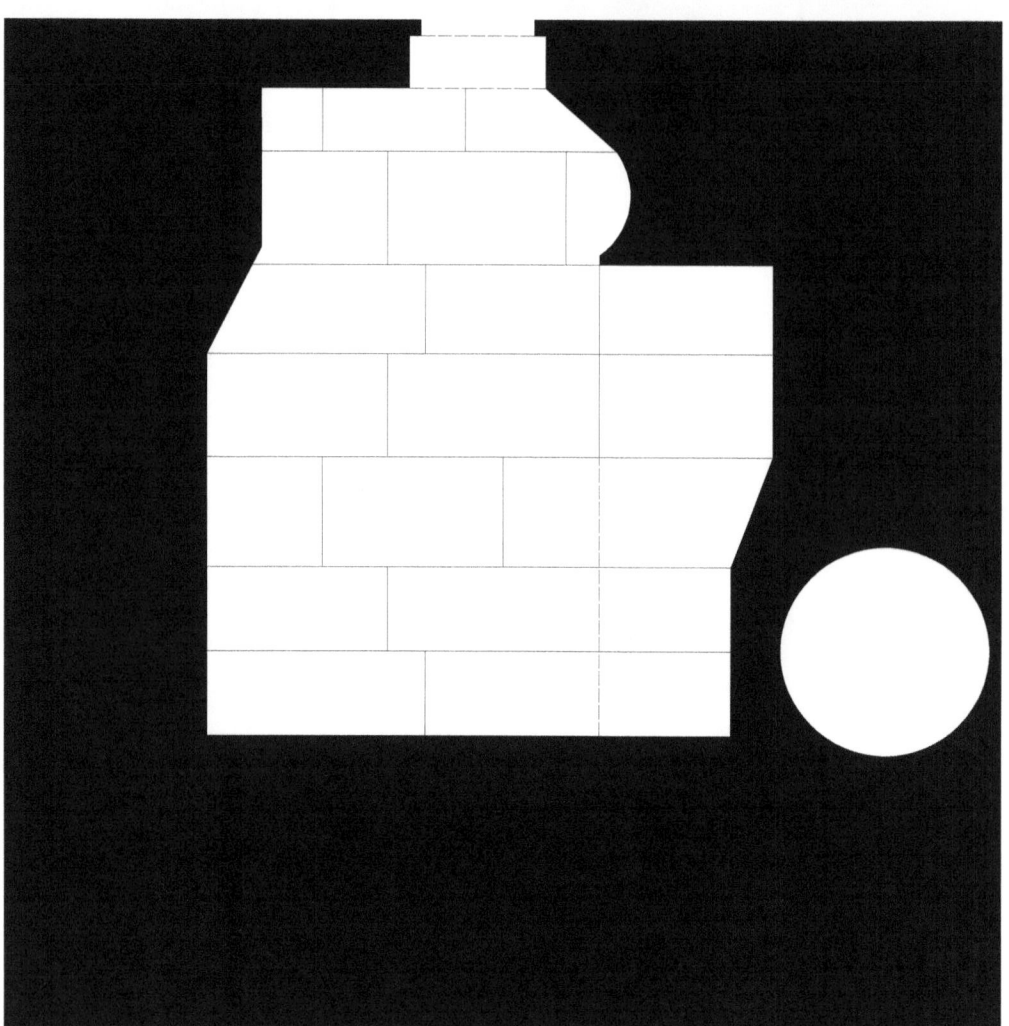

Tatev Monastery, Syunik, Armenia

Kye Monastery
Spiti, India

Kye Monastery, dedicated to Lochen Tulku, was founded in the 11th century by Dromtön. It rests atop the peak of a hill in the Spiti Valley, about 14,000 feet above sea level. This gompa has held countless ceremonies alongside the hundreds of lamas that have received their religious training here. Attacks by Mongol barbarians led to constant reconstruction. In order to lead peaceful lives they eventually created the erratic patchwork of rooms, tight hallways, and hidden courtyards that exist today.

Embedded in the landscape, seamlessly integrated, is a nucleated settlement structure. A perfectly preserved mountainous hill peak adorns a winding spiritual path one must take to happen upon the main gompa. Superimposed into the design is the carving of massing that had to happen to adorn this grouping, allowing for the stepping of each subsequent building to be timeless. The gentle placement, proportion and scale of each individual volume resonates with the existing nature, resulting in a geometrized mountain where the boundaries between architecture and nature dissolve.

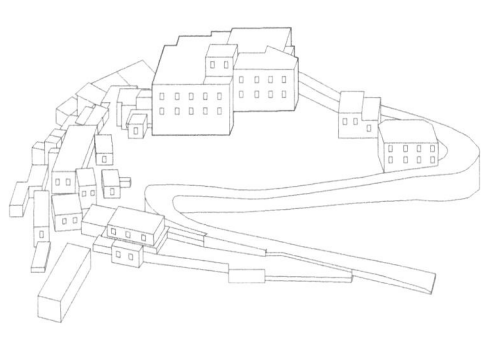

Kye Monastery, Spiti, India

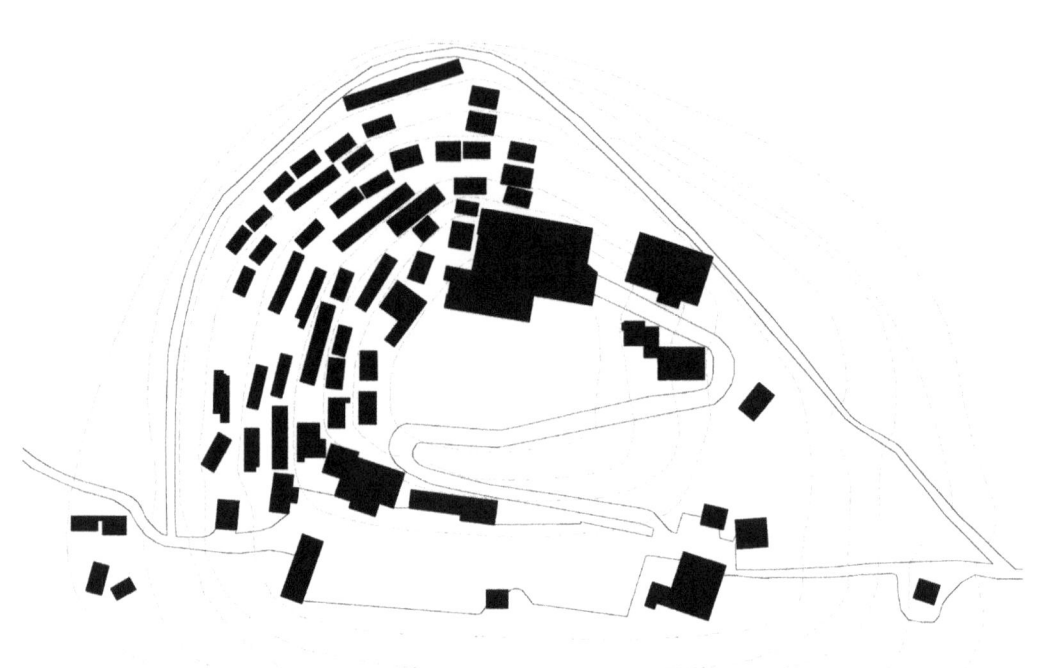

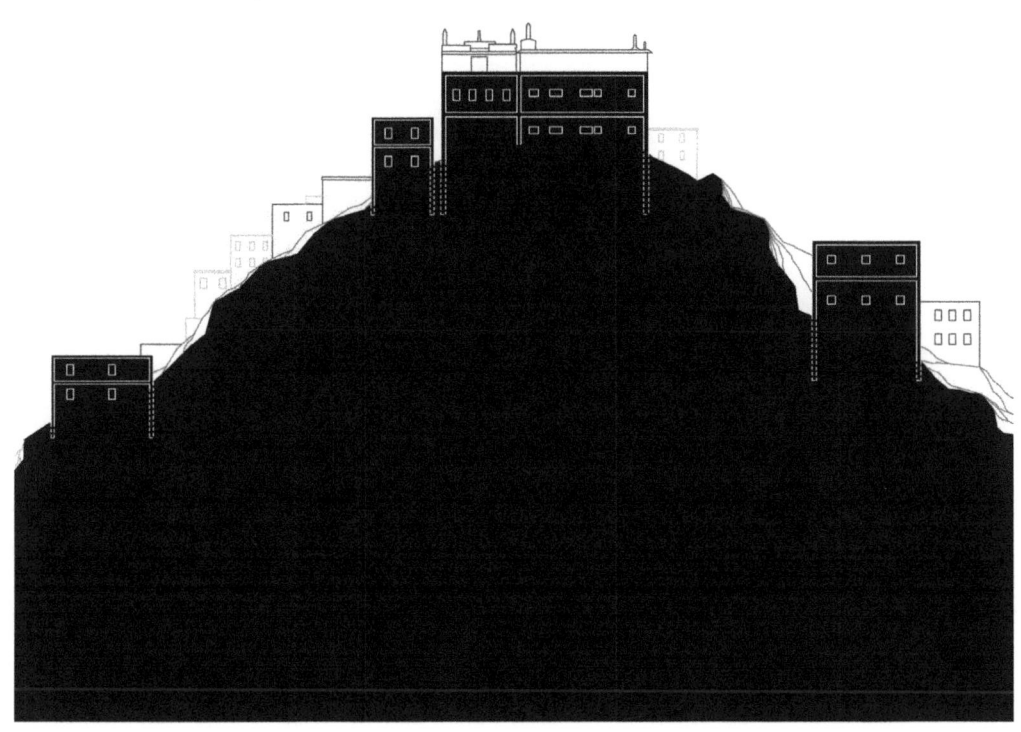

Kye Monastery, Spiti, India

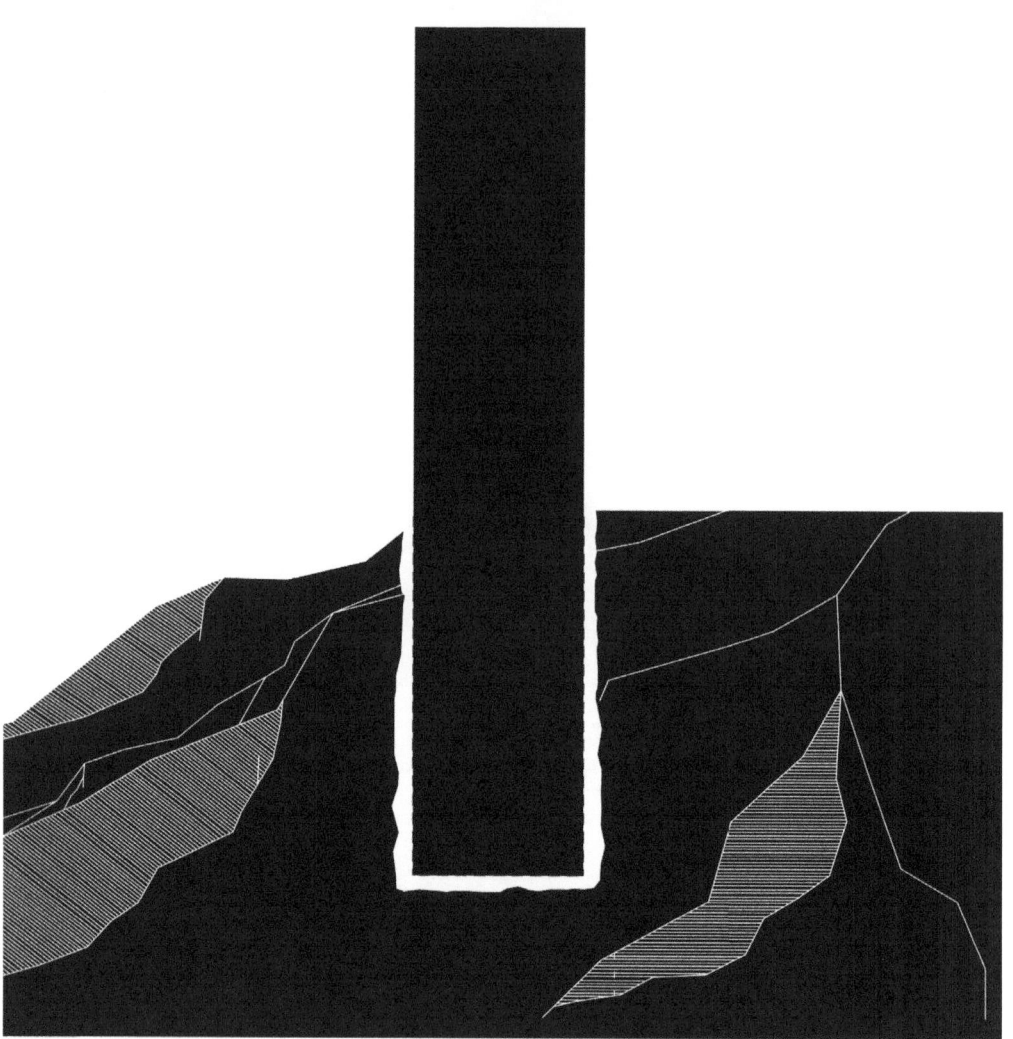

Architectural Precedents | Historic Case Studies

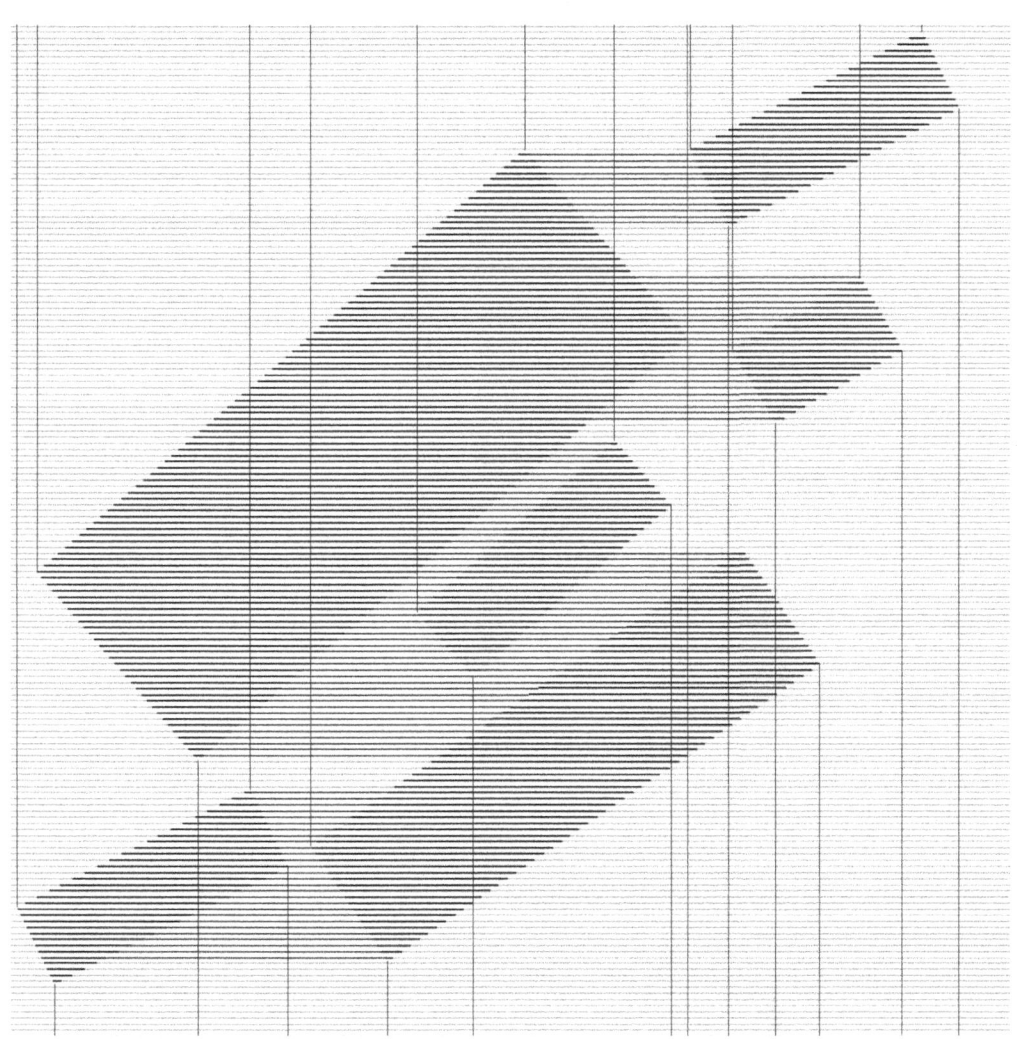

Kye Monastery, Spiti, India

**Simonos Petras Monastery
Athos, Greece**

Simonos Petras Monastery, founded in the 13th century by Hosios Simon the Athonite, rests upon Mount Athos among 19 other monasteries that emphasize the Eastern Orthodox Church teachings. The founder was sanctioned as Simon the Myrrh-bearer after Theotokos instructed him to build this monastery on top of this mountainous peak. The structure has persevered through the ages, even with the multiple fires that have brought it down, still holding portions of the original building.

The main structure is built as an extension of the precipitous rock terrain, while integrating itself onto it. Allowing for a subtle interplay between nature and built architecture. Each of the individual volumes is open to each other, creating a sequence of enclosed exterior courtyards, which can be read as a natural progression into intimacy. The section conveys an interesting dialog between conceptually stereotomic and tectonic spaces.

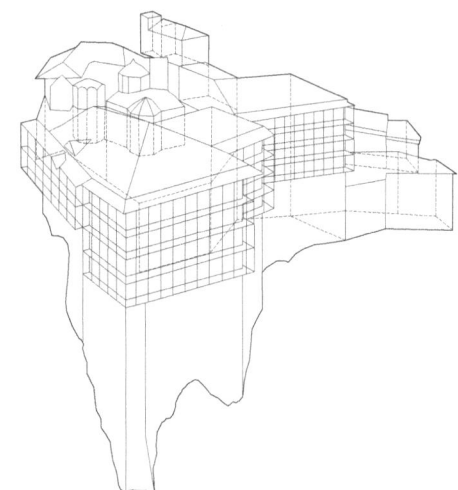

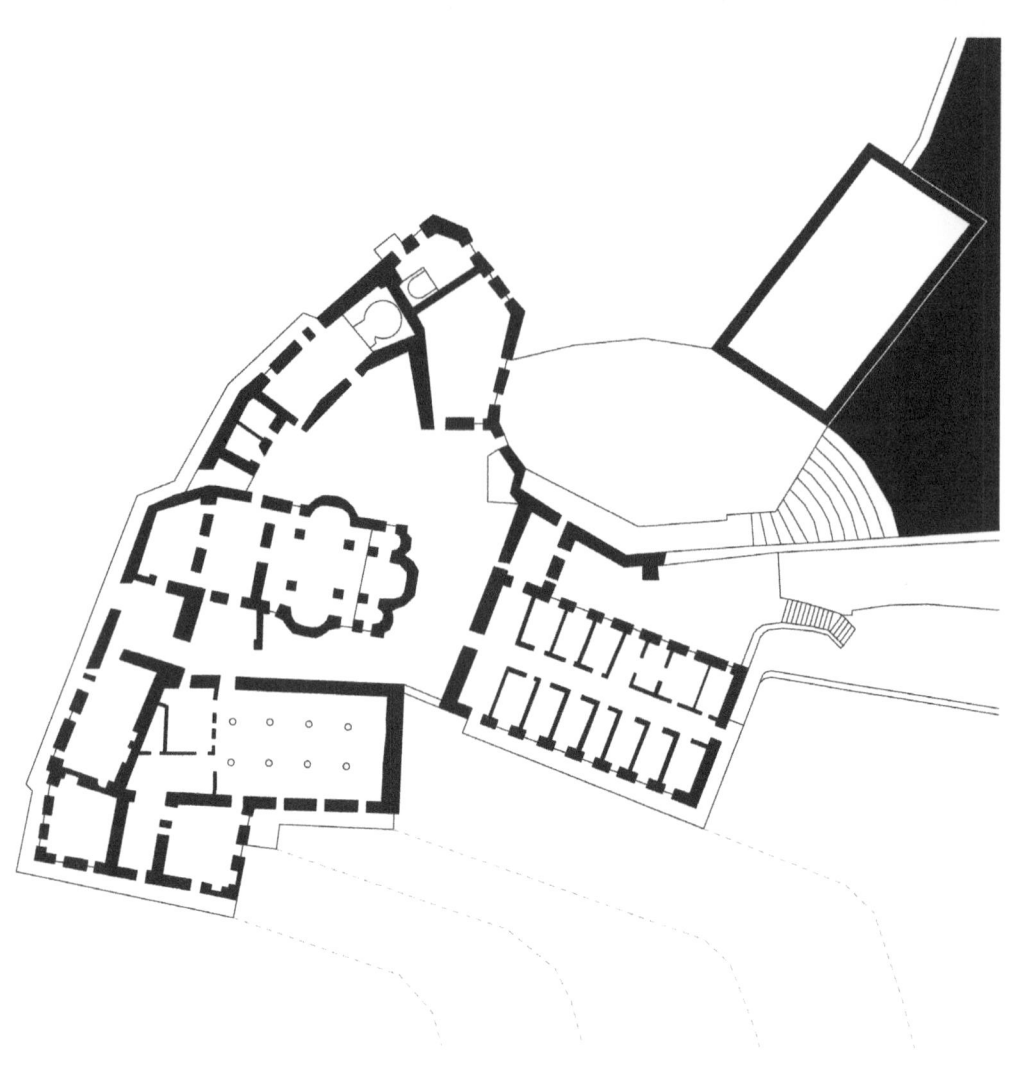

Simonos Petras Monastery, Athos, Greece   193

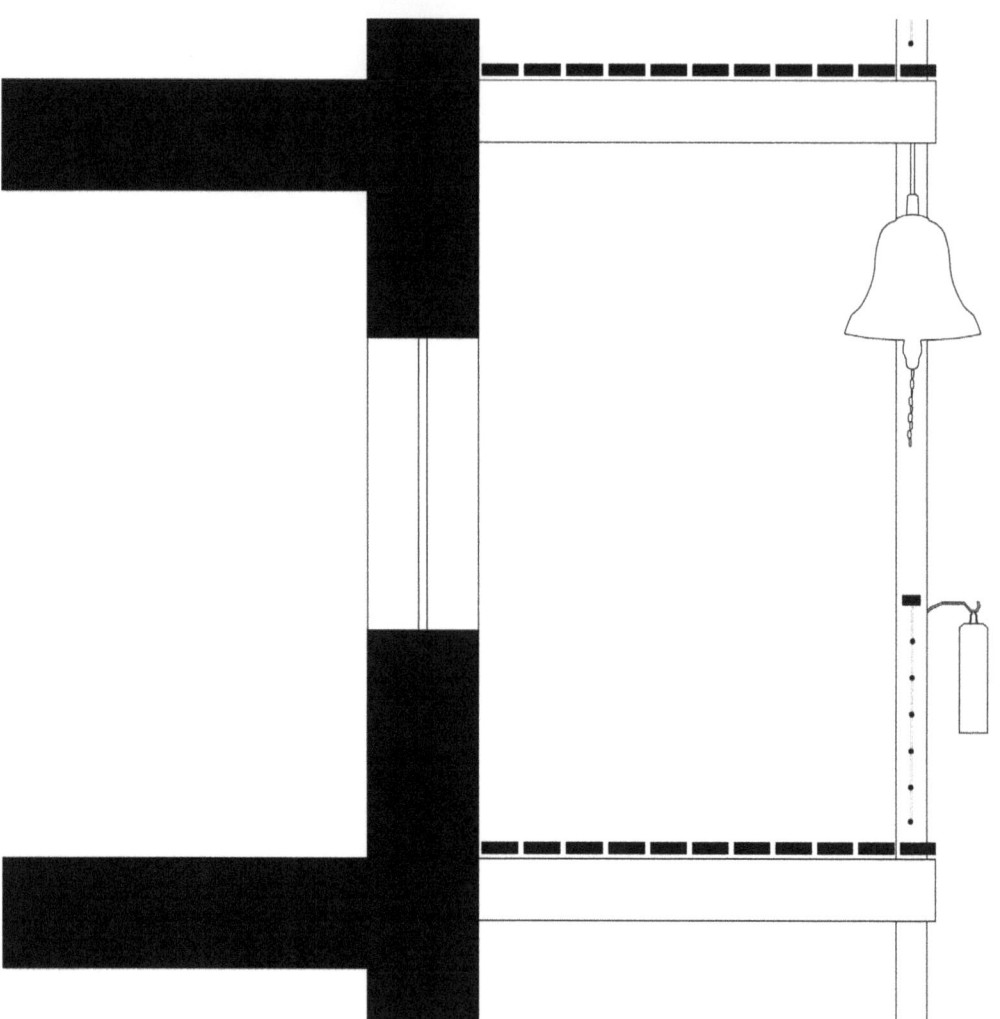

Simonos Petras Monastery, Athos, Greece

Phugtal Monastery
Ladakh, India

Phugtal Monastery sits isolated in the Lungkak Valley of Ladakh, India. It was built in the 12th century as a Buddhist monastery inserted into the cliffside, adorned over the Tsarap River. Said to have been created from a miracle produced by Jangsem Sherap Zangpo, a disciple of the founder of Tibetan Buddhism. The commune has grown over time from older rooms that were built around natural caves, into a complex system of interlocked essential volumes and structures.

The small scale of each of the individual volumes contrasts with the extended nature of the public space which is created between them. The presence of the waterfall, which emerges from a deeper cave, defines the mutable character of the constructed elements, which inevitably will be transformed by erosion.

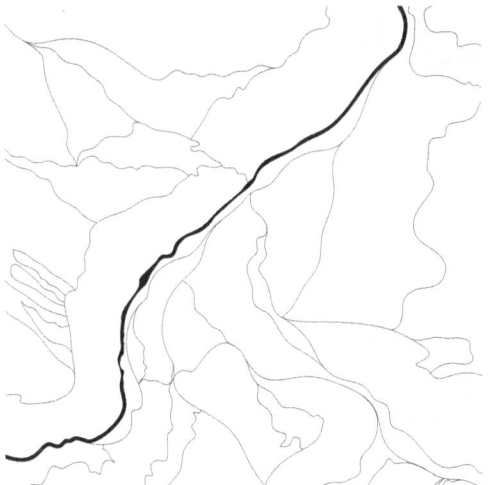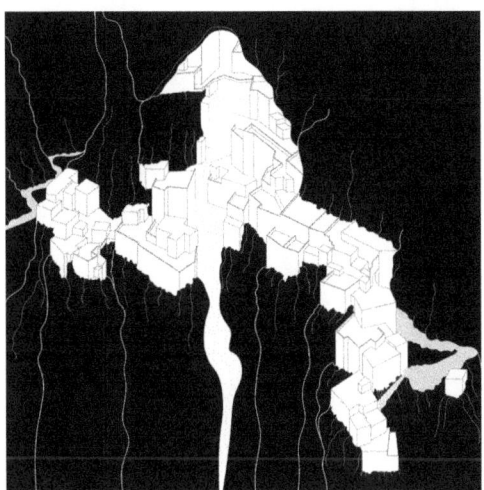

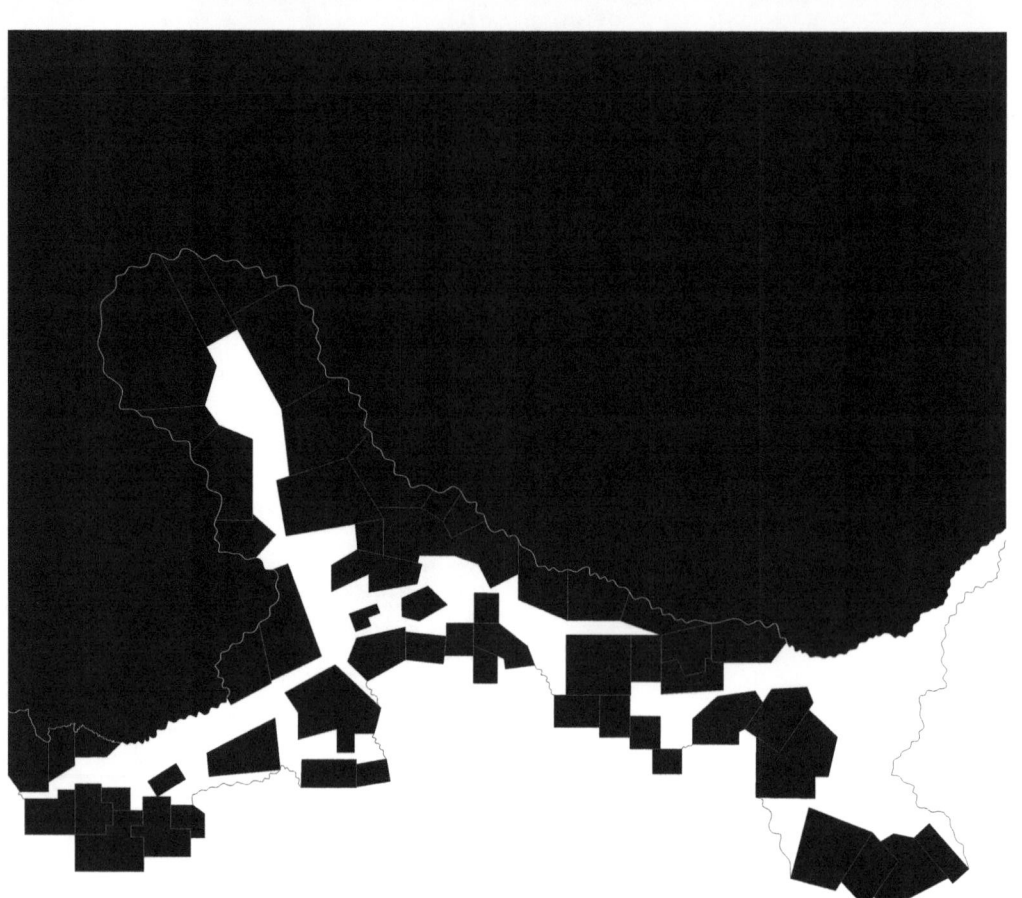

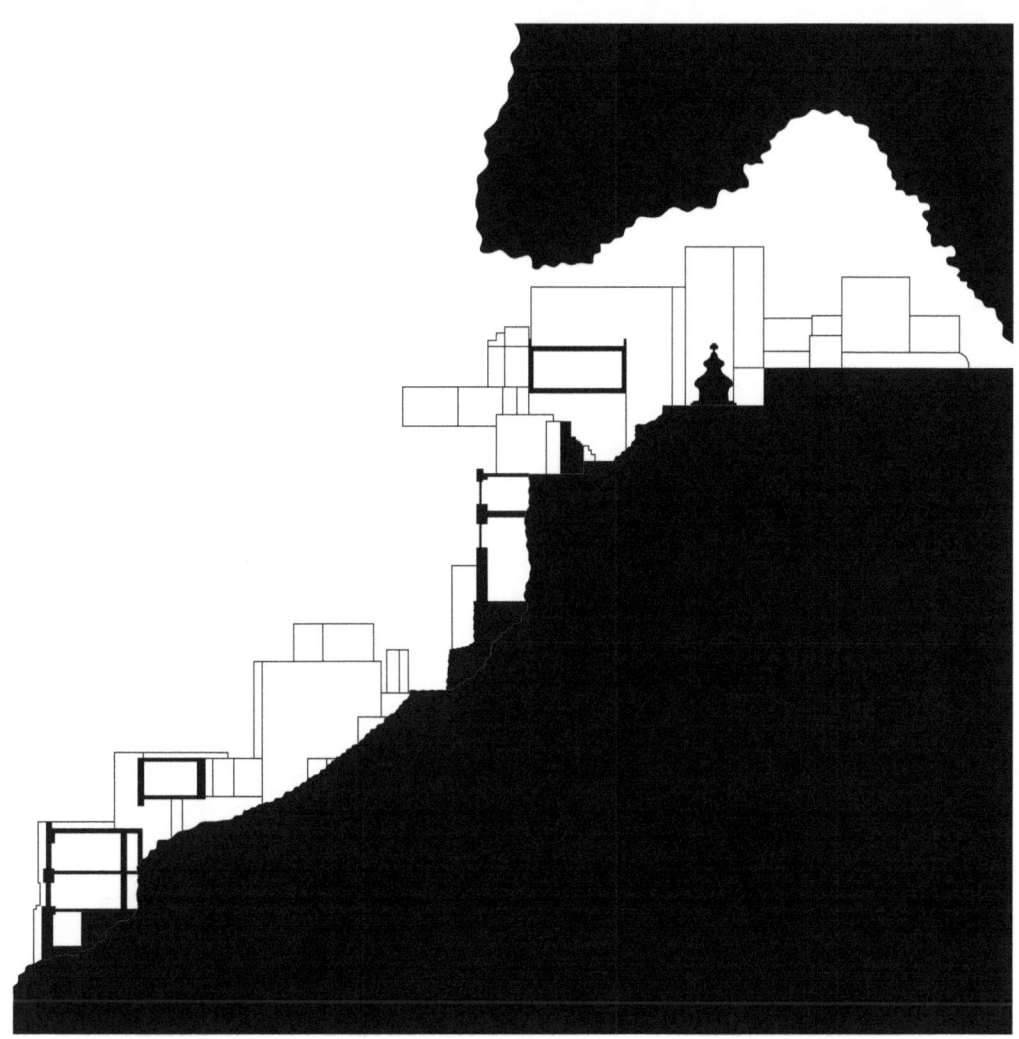

Architectural Precedents | Historic Case Studies

Visovac Monastery
Brištane, Croatia

Visovac Monastery is located ashore the island of Visovac in the heart of Krka National Park in Brištane, Croatia. Established in the 14th century by Augustinian monks, was dedicated to the Apostle Paul. This island was a place of nearly full isolation where young men prepared themselves for priesthood. This monastery is a key figure in the identity of Croatia, possessing a significant archaeological collection and a valuable rich library that acts as a fortress of spirituality and faith.

The full island is conceived as an isolated reduct, where the exterior spaces, paths and layered boundaries of dense vegetation become the actual monastery. The actual construction, very traditional in its nature, becomes secondary. The perimeter of the island is adjusted with rational geometry, acknowledging that the edge which separates land from water is the final boundary of the complex.

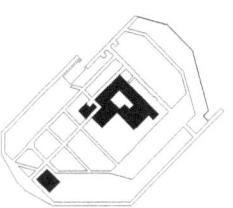
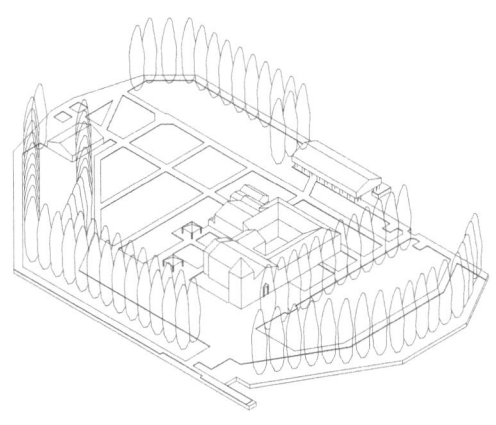

Visovac Monastery, Brištane, Croatia

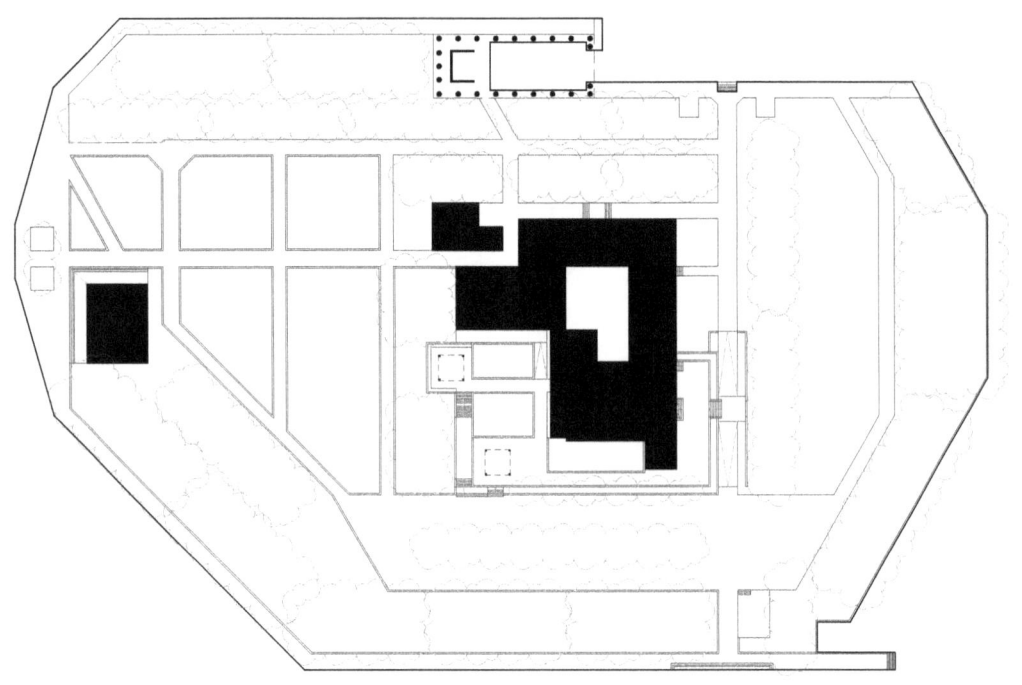

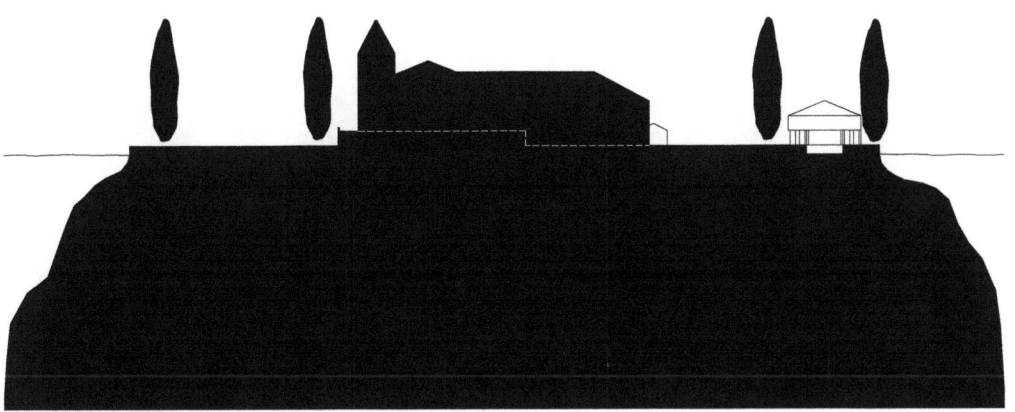

Visovac Monastery, Brištane, Croatia

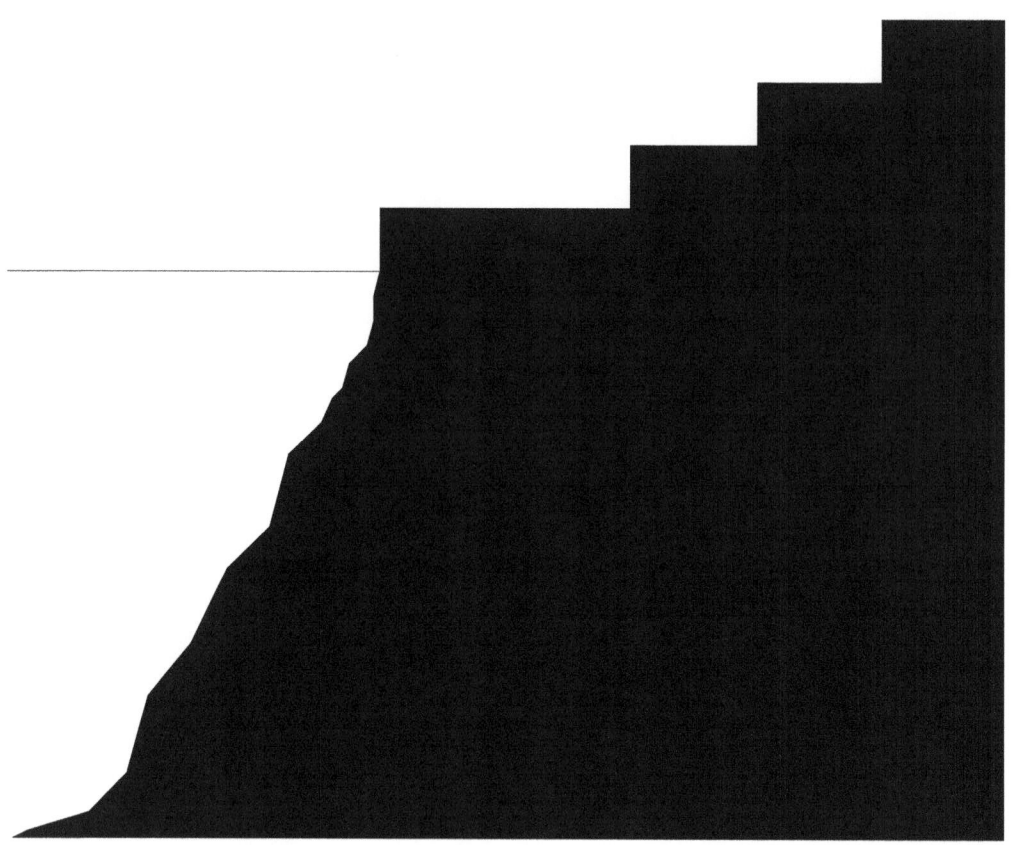

Architectural Precedents | Historic Case Studies

Ostrog Monastery
Ostroška Greda, Montenegro

Ostrog Monastery is placed within a sliver of an enormous rock on the Ostroška Greda, in Montenegro, and was founded by Vasilije, the Bishop of Herzegovina in the 17th century. This monastery is dedicated to Saint Basil of Ostrog, it was carved into the cliffside to protect itself from the Ottoman Empire incursions. It is layered into two distinct areas: the upper section that houses the Church of Presentation and the Church of the Holy Cross, and the lower section that houses the Church of the Holy Trinity.

Similarly to San Colombano, Ostrog fills with constructed elements an existing void in the mountain side. The vertical nature of the void makes that, in this occasion, the construction includes an extended set of stairs and platforms, redefining the mountain face as a geometric composition. The exterior wall of the monastery is nearly flush with the projected side of the mountain, as if restituting the natural cave with architecture.

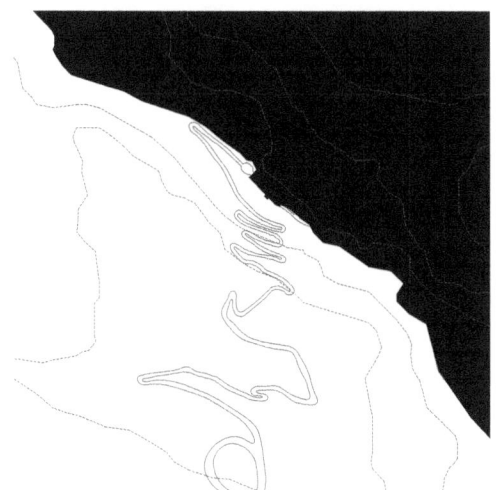

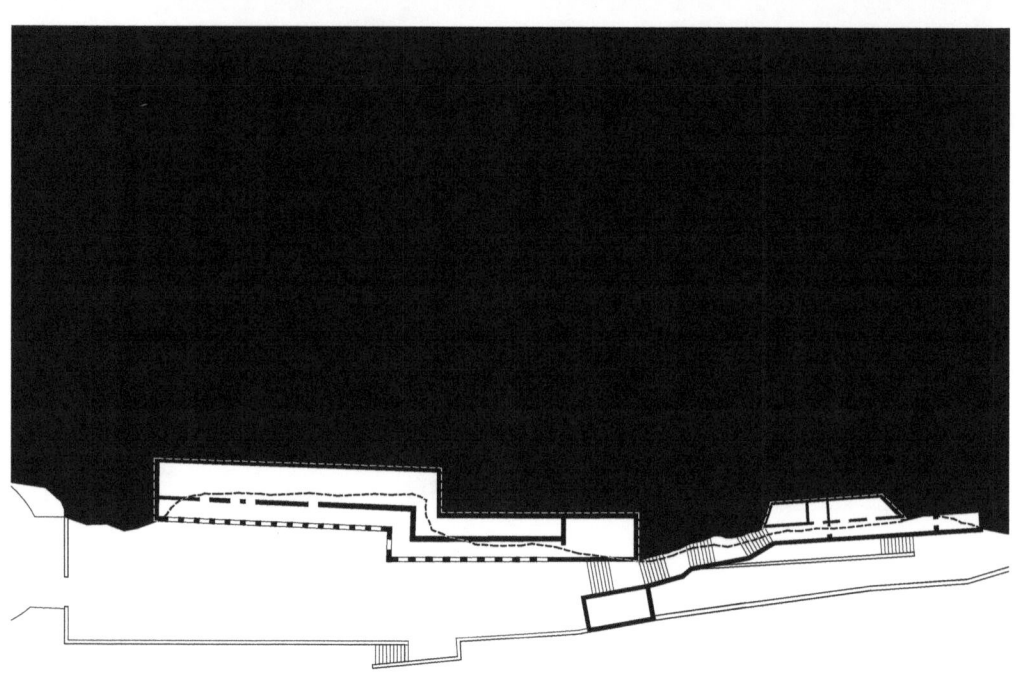

Architectural Precedents | Historic Case Studies

This is an academic publication, and the drawings included in this volume have been produced during the research phase of Graduate Design Studios Arch.515, which took place at the Cummings School of Architecture, Roger Williams University, during the fall semesters of 2022, 2023 and 2024, guided by Rubén Alcolea, Professor of Architecture.

This publication has been possible thanks to the support of Roger Williams University through its Professional Development Fund and the Graduate Assistantship Program.

Edited by
Rubén Alcolea

Layout, text and illustration editing by
Mauricio Escalante

Cover images
Tattershall Castle, by Mauricio Escalante
Orford Castle, by Noah Ellingwood

Backcover image
Deal Castle, by Garrett Doidge

British Castles

Peveril Castle, Castleton, England
1066-1086 C.E.
53.339960, -1.777516
Drawings by Nathan Cormier

Dover Castle, Kent, England
1066 - 1087 C.E.
51.129593, 1.321283
Drawings by Ethan Izzo

Hedingham Castle, Essex, England
1130 - 1140 C.E.
51.992512, 0.601437
Drawings by Audrey Barnhart

Orford Castle, Suffolk, England
1165 - 1173 C.E.
Orford Castle
Drawings by Noah Ellingwood

Trim Castle, Meath, Ireland
1172 C.E.
53.554321, -6.789738
Drawings by Emily Soares

Tattershall Castle, Lincolnshire, England
1231 - 1434 C.E.
53.101392, -0.193345
Drawings by Mauricio Escalante

Crichton Castle, Midlothian, Scotland
14th c. C.E.
55.839580, -2.991398
Drawings by Grace Salisbury

Borthwick Castle, Gorebridge, Scotland
1430 C.E.
55.826681, -3.007377
Drawings by Helena Mott

Walmer Castle, Kent, England
1539 - 1540 C.E.
51.200595, 1.402112
Drawings by Maria Cruz

Deal Castle, Kent, England
1539 - 1540 C.E.
51.219465, 1.403683
Drawings by Garrett Doidge

Spanish Castles

Peñafiel Castle, Valladolid, Spain
947 - 1013 C.E.
41.596937, -4.114416
Drawings by Niccola Zona

Burgalimar Castle, Jaén, Spain
967 C.E.
38.170319, -3.775492
Drawings by Ethan Medeiros

Javier Castle, Navarra, Spain
10th c. C.E.
42.594092, -1.215805
Drawings by Andrew Gouveia

Loarre Castle, Huesca, Spain
12th c. C.E.
42.325628, -0.612459
Drawings by Christos Moustopoulos

Villena Castle, Alicante, Spain
12th c. C.E.
38.631895, -0.861090
Drawings by Joseph DePoalo

Bellver Castle, Mallorca, Spain
1311 C.E.
39.563817, 2.619319
Drawings by Brennan Dunn

Butrón Castle, Vizcaya, Spain
14th c. C.E.
43.371700, -2.914247
Drawings by Ryan Duryea

Coca Castle, Segovia, Spain
1453 C.E.
41.215167, -4.525515
Drawings by Abbey Gilligan

Belmonte Castle, Cuenca, Spain
1456 C.E.
39.557942, -2.696967
Drawings by Rosh Walsh

Manzanares El Real Castle, Madrid, Spain
1475 C.E.
40.725464, -3.869713
Drawings by Marissa Lagoja

Belalcázar Castle, Córdoba, Spain
15th c. C.E.
38.582807, -5.165577
Drawings by Sophia Rotar-Crowe

Eastern Monasteries

Sümela Monastery, Karadağ, Turkey
386 C.E.
40.690083, 39.658375
Drawings by Caroline Keller

Saint Catherine Monastery, South Sinai, Egypt
548 - 565 C.E.
28.555931, 33.976083
Drawings by Julio Romero

Debre Damo, Northern Tigray, Ethiopia
6th c. C.E.
14.372467, 39.289144
Drawings by Stefan Cole

Tatev Monastery, Syunik, Armenia
848 - 906 C.E.
39.379278, 46.250434
Drawings by Evamarie Alessandroni

Kye Monastery, Spiti, India
1008 - 1064 C.E.
32.297757, 78.011989
Drawings by Justine Aho

Simonos Petras Monastery, Athos, Greece
1257 - 1368 C.E.
40.190363, 24.247028
Drawings by Carlye Cording

Phugtal Monastery, Ladakh, India
15th c. C.E.
33.268149, 77.179453
Drawings by Grace Noonan

Visovac Monastery, Brištane, Croatia
1576 C.E.
43.861082, 15.973258
Drawings by Marc Spera

Ostrog, Ostroška Greda, Montenegro
17th c. C.E.
42.674814, 19.030450
Drawings by Ryan Lehane